Maker Innovations Series

Jump start your path to discovery with the Apress Maker Innovations series! From the basics of electricity and components through to the most advanced options in robotics and Machine Learning, you'll forge a path to building ingenious hardware and controlling it with cutting-edge software. All while gaining new skills and experience with common toolsets you can take to new projects or even into a whole new career.

The Apress Maker Innovations series offers projects-based learning, while keeping theory and best processes front and center. So you get hands-on experience while also learning the terms of the trade and how entrepreneurs, inventors, and engineers think through creating and executing hardware projects. You can learn to design circuits, program AI, create IoT systems for your home or even city, and so much more!

Whether you're a beginning hobbyist or a seasoned entrepreneur working out of your basement or garage, you'll scale up your skillset to become a hardware design and engineering pro. And often using low-cost and open-source software such as the Raspberry Pi, Arduino, PIC microcontroller, and Robot Operating System (ROS). Programmers and software engineers have great opportunities to learn, too, as many projects and control environments are based in popular languages and operating systems, such as Python and Linux.

If you want to build a robot, set up a smart home, tackle assembling a weather-ready meteorology system, or create a brand-new circuit using breadboards and circuit design software, this series has all that and more! Written by creative and seasoned Makers, every book in the series tackles both tested and leading-edge approaches and technologies for bringing your visions and projects to life.

More information about this series at https://link.springer.com/bookseries/17311.

Record Weather Data with Arduino and Solar Power

Use Sensors to Record and Analyze Meteorological Data

Chunyan Li

Apress®

Record Weather Data with Arduino and Solar Power: Use Sensors to Record and Analyze Meteorological Data

Chunyan Li
BATON ROUGE, USA

ISBN-13 (pbk): 979-8-8688-0813-5   ISBN-13 (electronic): 979-8-8688-0814-2
https://doi.org/10.1007/979-8-8688-0814-2

Copyright © 2024 by Chunyan Li

This work is subject to copyright. All rights are reserved by the Publisher, whether the whole or part of the material is concerned, specifically the rights of translation, reprinting, reuse of illustrations, recitation, broadcasting, reproduction on microfilms or in any other physical way, and transmission or information storage and retrieval, electronic adaptation, computer software, or by similar or dissimilar methodology now known or hereafter developed.

Trademarked names, logos, and images may appear in this book. Rather than use a trademark symbol with every occurrence of a trademarked name, logo, or image we use the names, logos, and images only in an editorial fashion and to the benefit of the trademark owner, with no intention of infringement of the trademark.

The use in this publication of trade names, trademarks, service marks, and similar terms, even if they are not identified as such, is not to be taken as an expression of opinion as to whether or not they are subject to proprietary rights.

While the advice and information in this book are believed to be true and accurate at the date of publication, neither the authors nor the editors nor the publisher can accept any legal responsibility for any errors or omissions that may be made. The publisher makes no warranty, express or implied, with respect to the material contained herein.

Managing Director, Apress Media LLC: Welmoed Spahr
Acquisitions Editor: Susan McDermott
Development Editor: James Markham
Project Manager: Jessica Vakili

Distributed to the book trade worldwide by Springer Science+Business Media New York, 1 NY Plaza, New York, NY 10004. Phone 1-800-SPRINGER, fax (201) 348-4505, e-mail orders-ny@springer-sbm.com, or visit www.springeronline.com. Apress Media, LLC is a California LLC and the sole member (owner) is Springer Science + Business Media Finance Inc (SSBM Finance Inc). SSBM Finance Inc is a **Delaware** corporation.

For information on translations, please e-mail booktranslations@springernature.com; for reprint, paperback, or audio rights, please e-mail bookpermissions@springernature.com.

Apress titles may be purchased in bulk for academic, corporate, or promotional use. eBook versions and licenses are also available for most titles. For more information, reference our Print and eBook Bulk Sales web page at http://www.apress.com/bulk-sales.

Any source code or other supplementary material referenced by the author in this book is available to readers on the Github repository: https://github.com/Apress/Record-Weather-Data-with-Arduino-and-Solar-Power. For more detailed information, please visit https://www.apress.com/gp/services/source-code.

If disposing of this product, please recycle the paper

For the days, dark or bright
For the ocean, this shore and that side
For the dreams, like a child like a star
For the journey, easy or harsh ...

Table of Contents

About the Author

Chunyan Li is a professor teaching oceanography and meteorology at Louisiana State University. He has made dozens of weather recording units powered by battery or solar panels for research projects and student projects. He has published more than 140 scientific research papers, coauthored a book titled *Meteorology for Coastal Scientists* and authored another book titled *Time Series Data Analysis in Oceanography - Applications using MATLAB*. He is also the director of a research lab of an offshore meteorology and oceanography observation system for weather, waves, tides, currents, and storm surges, as part of the Gulf of Mexico Coastal Ocean Observing System (GCOOS). His research includes theories, observations, and applications of coastal and estuarine dynamics under the influence of tides, rivers, and weather, as well as impacts of climate change on the Arctic and subtropical coastal oceans.

About the Technical Reviewer

Roland Meisel holds a B.Sc. in physics from the University of Windsor, a B.Ed. from Queen's University specializing in physics and mathematics, and an M.Sc. in physics from the University of Waterloo. He worked at Chalk River Nuclear Laboratories before entering the world of education. He spent 28 years teaching physics, mathematics, and computer science in the Ontario secondary school system. After retiring from teaching as the Head of Mathematics at Ridgeway Crystal Beach High School, he entered the world of publishing, contributing to mathematics and physics texts from pre-algebra to calculus in various roles including technology consultant and author of interactive web files, and photography. He remains active in several organizations including the Ontario Association of Physics Teachers, the Ontario Association of Mathematics Educators, the Canadian Owners and Pilots Association, and the Wainfleet Historical Society.

Acknowledgments

I extend my gratitude to ExxonMobil Corporation for their support through the ExxonMobil Distinguished Professorship at Louisiana State University. This professorship has been instrumental in allowing me to experiment with electronics and develop self-built weather stations in southern Louisiana and the Arctic, leading to the creation of this book. As a college professor in oceanography and meteorology, I am not an electronics expert but have learned to experiment with sensors and electronics with curiosity and respect, applying some of my ideas to research projects.

I also thank Jessica Vakili at Apress for her support in writing this book. Despite delays due to my research and teaching commitments, her patience and encouragement enabled me to complete the manuscript.

Preface

Target Audience and Applications

This book is designed for students, hobbyists, science teachers, and anyone keen on creating a solar-powered weather data recorder using Arduino, a widely used electronics development board. It covers the step-by-step process of building weather recording sensor packages utilizing Arduino microcontrollers, weather sensors, and solar power. These sensor packages can be used to record weather conditions or be used for postanalysis related to atmospheric events like tropical cyclones, cold fronts, or even tornadoes (though rare). The air pressure sensors are also capable of detecting large volcanic eruptions and explosions (also very rare). For instance, my own handmade devices successfully recorded the catastrophic Tonga underwater volcanic explosion on January 15, 2022, from over 10,600 km away, capturing global-scale atmospheric shockwaves. The sensor packages described can also be adapted for various other purposes.

Safety Precautions

The projects described in this book involve using batteries, AC electricity, soldering irons, heat guns, wire cutters, glue guns, and other tools. Exercise caution when working with electrical, thermal, and mechanical tools. Ensure adequate ventilation when soldering to avoid inhaling toxic fumes, and wear goggles for protection. Minors should not undertake these projects alone and should always be supervised by knowledgeable adults.

Working on Electronic Projects

Engaging in electronic projects can be challenging, requiring not only a grasp of the overall design but also meticulous attention to detail, patience in debugging (resolving code errors), and perseverance in overcoming difficult problems. The projects in this book involve writing or modifying Arduino scripts. All the codes I provided here were tested and work with the sensors or components involved. Despite the provided codes, numerous factors can affect performance or determine if the setup will work, such as the proper installation of sensor libraries. Fortunately, the latest Arduino IDE versions simplify finding and installing these libraries. Other critical factors include wiring, sensor and component quality, and soldering skills. Sometimes, even with meticulous efforts, the setup may not work initially. In such cases, persistence and perseverance are key to eventual success.

To make the experience of doing the projects more enjoyable and reduce potential frustration, I recommend an incremental approach, especially for beginners working with Arduino or complex projects involving multiple sensors and components. This method involves starting with individual components and gradually adding more components and integrating them. For example, begin by connecting and testing a GPS module with Arduino. Once successful, add a liquid crystal display, followed by an SD card. This incremental approach, used throughout this book, helps build confidence and ensures functionality before combining all elements into the final product.

Book Structure

This book demonstrates several hands-on projects for assembling sensor packages using Arduino microcontrollers and solar power to record weather data. Chapter 1 serves as an introduction, showcasing several exciting success stories from my own work as examples. Chapter 2 covers an introduction to solar power and steps to connect a solar panel to a battery and electric load, which in our case is a weather data recorder. Chapter 3 provides general information about Arduino microcontrollers. Chapter 4 details working with a GPS module to collect geolocation and time data. Chapter 5 explains using liquid crystal displays to facilitate sensor-user communication. Chapter 6 introduces SD cards for data storage and postevent analysis. Chapter 7 focuses on creating a GPS recorder. Chapter 8 introduces air pressure, temperature, and humidity sensors. Finally, Chapter 9 integrates all sensors and an Arduino board together with solar power as the energy source for deployment and measurements.

CHAPTER 1

Introduction

1.1. Background

I consider myself one of the many explorers of nature, investigating its behavior and mechanisms. Such explorations can have many different aspects, emphases, and approaches, using various tools. Professionally, I am a college professor who studies and teaches the natural physical processes in ocean water and atmosphere. My background combines meteorology and oceanography. Most of my work involves studying the movement of water in the ocean and estuaries under various forcing factors, such as astronomical tides and weather.

To simplify, I often use the phrase "meteorology in the water" (dynamical oceanography) to explain my studies in the ocean. Meteorology is the study of weather, focusing on a few commonly known quantities such as wind speed, wind direction, air pressure, air temperature, humidity, and air density, which are key factors in understanding air movement (horizontal wind and vertical convection) and associated weather events. In the study of "meteorology in water," the water level above a given depth determines the water pressure at that depth, analogous to air pressure. The temperature of ocean water corresponds to air temperature, ocean salinity corresponds to humidity in the air (both crucial in determining density), water density corresponds to air density, and ocean current corresponds to wind.

© Chunyan Li 2024
C. LI, *Record Weather Data with Arduino and Solar Power*, Maker Innovations Series,
https://doi.org/10.1007/979-8-8688-0814-2_1

Using this simple analogy, the quantities involved in the study of "meteorology in water" are similar to those in meteorology. Both studies are largely based on fluid mechanics, derived from the classical Newton's laws, calculus, and differential equations in mathematics. In both oceanography and meteorology, the theories are the fundamental laws and the mathematics are the tools. However, these are not sufficient without measurements: studies in both the atmosphere and ocean heavily depend on measurements.

Events occur in nature constantly, and it is important to monitor and record them to respond promptly or study them to better prepare for and mitigate potential damage. Over the years, I have used various scientific apparatuses for measurements, which are often expensive for an ordinary person to acquire. Despite the ease of access to scientific tools on the market, I have been interested in making my own devices or sensor packages as a hobby to record data. Although I am not a professional electronics expert, I have tinkered with electronics projects after work, utilizing Arduino microcontrollers and inexpensive sensors to create simple devices that have recorded useful data over at least the past 12 years at various locations for different objectives, including coastal Louisiana and the Arctic.

Among the packages I made, perhaps the most practical one is a solar-powered weather measurement package that includes a GPS, an SD card, a liquid crystal display (LCD), a pressure sensor that measures atmospheric pressure, a temperature sensor that measures air temperature, a humidity sensor that measures relative humidity, and an ultrasonic anemometer that measures wind direction and speed (Figure 1-1). The device can be programmed to measure and record data at predetermined intervals, up to every second. Over the years, I have made dozens of similar packages, some with and some without the ultrasonic anemometer, as the anemometer is relatively expensive (a few thousand dollars). Figure 1-1 shows my weather station, assembled using an Arduino board and sensors, including an ultrasonic anemometer, mounted on a pole in the Arctic during a study funded by the North Pacific Research Board.

Figure 1-1. *A solar-powered weather station assembled by the author and deployed in the Arctic (Barrow, Alaska)*

With this experience and background, especially assembling handmade devices using Arduino microprocessors, I am compiling relevant information in this book to help people like me and anyone interested in recording weather information using their own handmade solar-powered sensors. I hope these projects are inspiring and provide as much enjoyment as I experienced working on them. The computer codes or scripts I present here are based on either open-source library examples or codes I wrote, modified, and/or integrated. While I have many years of experience programming in various computer languages, mostly for mathematical models for the ocean and computations in my everyday research, I am not a professional programmer for electronics, and code optimization is usually not my priority compared to producing a correct and practical product with a working algorithm. As a result, the projects presented here might not be fully optimized in terms of design and efficiency. I am sure many smart people can write more efficient codes. However, I provide a series of practical, working projects that lead to an integrated product for studying weather, based on my practice in obtaining weather data for research. There are books dedicated to detailed tutorials and instructions for working with Arduino boards, individual sensors, or components. This book focuses on integrating weather sensors powered by solar energy for continuous data recording.

1.2. An Example: Recording the Global Spherical Shockwaves from a Volcano Explosion

Here, I provide an example of the data I collected unexpectedly: the global spherical shockwaves propagating in the atmosphere generated by the Hunga Tonga-Hunga Ha'apai underwater volcanic explosion in January 2022. This is an example of recording a nonweather event using weather sensors. The spherical shockwave signals were recorded by two weather recorders I made and deployed in Louisiana, more than 10,600 km away from the volcano. Of course, these devices were not intended for recording a volcanic eruption, nor could anyone predict such an event many years in advance. This example shows how a simple handmade device can record useful environmental data during unexpected events. It should be noted that the shockwave signals from the Tonga underwater volcanic eruption were recorded at thousands of weather stations around the world, mostly at five-minute and one-minute intervals. The devices I made and deployed were recording at 3-second and 21-second intervals, respectively, providing details of the shockwaves that most weather stations could not capture.

1.2.1. The Volcanic Eruption

On January 15, 2022, a large eruption of the Hunga Tonga-Hunga Ha'apai underwater volcano occurred around or before 04:14:45 UTC (17:14:45 local time). This volcano is located in the Southern Pacific (20°33' S, 175°23'6" W), approximately 1,900 km north-northeast of New Zealand, 3,200 km east of Australia, and 600 km southeast of Fiji. The nearby islands of Hunga Tonga and Hunga Ha'apai, with an area of 1 km² and a maximum altitude of 149 m, were blown apart. Eruption-induced tsunami waves were observed in the Pacific Ocean, damaging at least 600 structures, including 300 residential buildings. The economic damage was estimated at greater than 90 million US dollars.

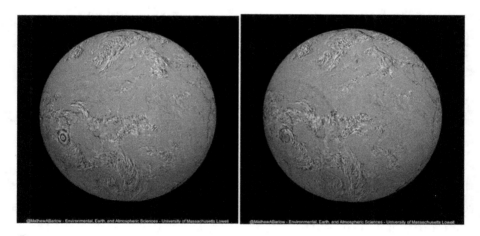

Figure 1-2. *Atmospheric spherical shockwaves from the Tonga volcanic eruption on Jan. 15, 2022 (captured from* `https://github.com/mathewbarlow/animations/blob/main/tonga_wave_labeled.gif`*)*

The explosion is believed to be a once-in-a-millennium event for the Hunga caldera. The eruption reached at least 35-45 km altitude, and transiently 58 km, creating shockwaves that propagated around the globe. These were captured by geostationary satellites, including NOAA's GEOS-17 and Japanese Himawari-8 (Figure 1-2), and were measured in Britain and Ireland up to 127 hours later. The eruption energy, estimated at 4-18 megatons, was below that of the Mount St. Helens (United States) explosion in 1980 (24 megatons) and the Krakatoa (Indonesia) explosion in 1883.

It is known that explosions such as volcanic eruptions can produce measurable atmospheric pressure waves at weather stations, and air pressure variations have been used to estimate the total energy from volcanic eruptions and man-made explosions, such as nuclear explosions. For example, using such data, the mysterious Siberian explosion at Tunguska in 1908 was studied, finding that the atmospheric shockwave produced by this explosion propagated at a speed of 285-324 m/s. The total energy was estimated at ~12.5 ± 2.5 megatons (1 megaton = 4.18 × 10^{15} joules) from an unknown source, possibly a meteorite hit. The difference in wave speed estimates was believed to be caused by different meteorological conditions at different stations.

1.2.2. The Shockwave Signal Recorded by Arduino Weather Stations

On January 15, 2022, two of my self-made solar-powered weather data loggers based on Arduino boards recorded abnormal air pressure changes caused by the explosion. These devices had been deployed at two stations for more than ten years. These stations are about 10,627 and 10,621 km from the volcano, respectively, and about 10 km apart. Figure 1-3 shows the air pressure data recorded at one of the stations. The shockwaves arrived from two routes in the atmosphere: the shortest spherical arc and the longer spherical arc through the antipole of the explosion. This led to two recorded signals, labeled as signal 1 and signal 2 (Figure 1-3). These signals travelled around the Earth multiple times, and many weather stations recorded them even up to the 6th pass of the signals around the Earth. Figure 1-4 shows a zoomed-in view of the two signals in Figure 1-3.

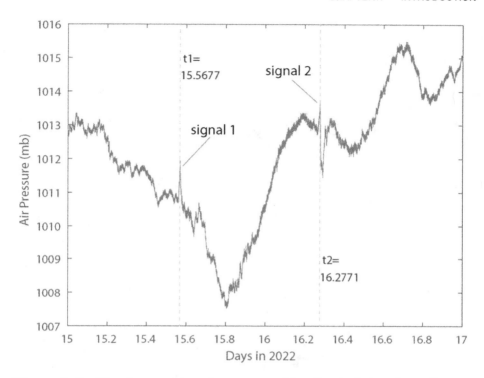

Figure 1-3. *Shockwave signals measured by the Arduino-based weather station*

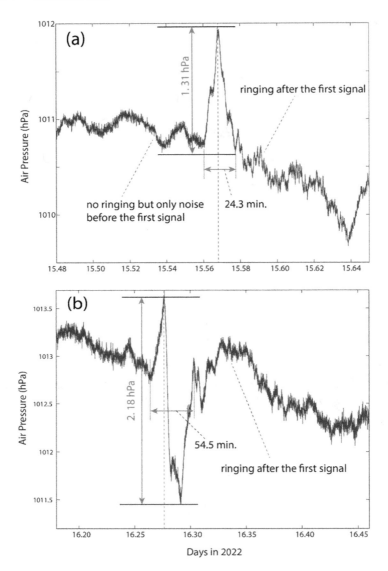

Figure 1-4. *A zoomed-in version of Figure 1-3 showing each of the two signals from the Tonga volcanic explosion occurred on Jan 15, 2022: (a) signal 1 and (b) signal 2 of Figure 1-3*

CHAPTER 2

Working with Solar Power

2.1. Solar Energy

The movements of the atmosphere and ocean are driven by the Sun through radiational heating and tide-generating force. In terms of the radiational heat input, if the Sun provides 100 units of radiation energy to the Earth, about 70 units are absorbed by the Earth, while the remaining 30 units are reflected by clouds and the Earth's surface back into space (the reflection rate, called albedo, is 0.3 for the Earth). Of the 70 units absorbed by the Earth, about 50 units are absorbed by a very thin layer (on the order of centimeter) of the Earth's surface, while the remaining 20 units are absorbed by the entire atmosphere, which has a thickness of tens of kilometers. In other words, most of the solar energy is absorbed by a thin layer of the Earth's surface. The 20 units of solar energy heating the atmosphere are spread thin over tens of kilometers. This makes the Earth's surface warmer than the atmosphere; the warmer surface then heats the atmosphere from the bottom up. As the air at the Earth's surface is heated, it expands and becomes lighter, causing it to rise and carry moisture from the surface. The rising air may then form clouds if there is enough moisture above the lifting condensation level. The surrounding air moves in to compensate for the lost air at the surface, producing wind and other

© Chunyan Li 2024
C. LI, *Record Weather Data with Arduino and Solar Power*, Maker Innovations Series,
https://doi.org/10.1007/979-8-8688-0814-2_2

weather phenomena. The wind also drives ocean currents (in addition to tidal currents). Living things on Earth depend on the Sun's energy: photosynthesis provides energy for plants, which are then consumed and used by animals in the food chain.

2.2. The Photoelectric Effect

Solar radiation energy consists of both visible and invisible lights, which are all electromagnetic waves. About 43% of this energy is in the visible band, 53% in the invisible infrared band, less than 5% in the ultraviolet radiation (invisible) band, and the remaining smallest (negligible) fraction in a band including X-ray and gamma rays.

One of the major advances of the last century is the technology to convert solar energy to electric energy. In 1887, a German physicist named Heinrich Rudolf Hertz observed that when ultraviolet radiation was applied to two metal electrodes, the voltage across them would change. Later in 1902, this phenomenon was further generalized when another German physicist, Philipp Lenard, showed that an illuminated metal surface would release electric particles. In general, when electromagnetic radiation is applied to certain material, electrons are released to form an electric current. This is called the *photoelectric effect*, one of the greatest discoveries of the late 19th and early 20th century, first explained in theory by Albert Einstein in 1905. The theory explained the photoelectric effect by photons, with the photon energy (E) being proportional to the frequency (f) of the electromagnetic wave: $E=hf$, in which h is the Planck constant ($6.62607015 \times 10^{-34}$ joules/Hz). Sixteen years later, Einstein won the Nobel prize for his contributions to theoretical physics, especially for his discovery of the law of the photoelectric effect.

Based on Einstein's theory, photovoltaic cells were invented to convert light to electricity. Solar panels are made using arrays of photovoltaic cells. In the following, we will demonstrate how to set up necessary components to use solar energy to run a small electric device such as a weather station.

2.3. Tools and Components

The basic tools and components needed in this chapter are listed in Table 2-1.

Table 2-1. *Components and tools used in Chapter 2*

Item	Description
30–40 W photovoltaic module (solar panel)	To convert solar power to electric power
A generic multimeter	For testing the voltage and currents, e.g., those from the solar panel
12 V nonspillable sealed lead acid $\geq$ 8 ampere-hour (Ah) battery (Ah is a measure of electric charge)	To be charged during the day and used during the nights or cloudy or rainy days [note: avoid any situation in which the positive and negative terminals of a battery may have a short circuit, e.g., a screwdriver or wire touching both positive and negative terminals]
12 V to 7 V or 12 V to 9 V step-down converter	Lower the DC voltage from the solar controller before applying to the Arduino board to reduce heat generation on the Arduino board
An outdoor waterproof enclosure (e.g., size ~11 in × 6.5 in × 6 in)	Housing for the Arduino board, solar controller, battery, GPS module, and sensors
Two cable glands	For protected connections with wire between the inside and outside of the enclosure
One bag of silica gel desiccant	For moisture reduction
A 12 V solar controller (e.g., the SunSaver-10L)	Controlling and stabilizing the output voltage from the solar panel

(continued)

Table 2-1. (*continued*)

Item	Description
Hole saw kit (should include 1 inch diameter cutter or one matching the diameter of the cable gland)	Cutting holes for the cable gland on the plastic or fiberglass enclosure for Arduino board, battery, solar controller, and possibly some sensors unless all sensors are housed in a separate solar radiation shield for better shielding from direct sunlight and better ventilation for more accurate temperature and humidity measurements
Power drill	For use with the hole cutter for the circular holes to install the cable glands
Wire stripper	For wire stripping. It can strip wires of different diameters
Spade terminals	To be used for connecting battery terminals. Female spade terminals are needed if the battery has two male terminals
Heat-shrink tubes	For insulation after soldering two wires together. Variable diameter heat-shrink tubes should be available for convenience
Heat gun	To heat the heat-shrink tubes for insulation [note: risk of burn and fire, use with extreme caution. Unplug after each use. Always keep flammable materials away from a heat gun. Never let a heat gun plugged in unattended]
Soldering station with some solder	For soldering wires to connect the DC-DC step-down converter to the 2.1 mm DC pigtail male power plug [note: an alternative approach without using the soldering station is to use wire nuts]
A 2.1 mm DC pigtail male power plug	This plug is to be used to connect the Arduino UNO with the DC power from the output end of the step-down converter

2.4. Solar Panel, Solar Controller, and Rechargeable Battery

Solar panels work based on the principles of the photoelectric effect: they convert solar (light) energy into electric energy in the form of direct current (DC), which can be used to run electronic devices outdoors where there is no power supply. This makes it very useful for an outdoor electronic device such as a weather station with various sensors. To run a small electronic device involving a few sensors for weather, a small rectangular solar panel of 30-40 W is usually sufficient for most applications.

Electronic devices usually require certain DC voltage and current to run properly. The operating voltage or current varies with the device. If the voltage or current is too low, the device will not run. On the other hand, too much voltage or current can potentially damage the electronics. Electric power (P) is measured by the product of the voltage (V, in volts) and current (I, in amperes), i.e., $P = IV$ (watts). A high voltage does not necessarily mean high power because the current might be weak. When working with an electronic device, we should keep in mind the requirements of power, voltage, and current. Each solar panel should have a designed voltage and power output.

The actual performance and power output from a specific solar panel, however, depends on many factors. For example, it depends on the available solar energy and the angle of installation of the solar panel. The available solar energy also depends on several other factors such as geolocation, which is fixed for any given site, the height of the Sun (a function of time of the year and time of the day), visibility of the sky, and cloud coverage. These factors, especially cloud coverage, change constantly. As a result, the voltage and output energy from a solar panel can fluctuate greatly. This fluctuation of energy makes it difficult for many electric devices to use and tolerate. To stabilize the output voltage, we need a voltage regulator (sometimes called a solar controller, Figure 2-1), which is an electronic device that helps to make the voltage constant.

Figure 2-1. *An example of a 10A/12 V solar controller. The two connections for "SOLAR" are to connect the positive and negative wires of the solar panel*

Additionally, we need a way to store solar energy during the day and use the stored energy at night. The general solution is to use a solar controller and a rechargeable battery to ensure a stable supply of energy, including at night and during times of heavy cloud coverage during the day. The solar panel runs the device during the day, and when there is an ample supply of solar energy, the excess energy is stored in the battery.

2.5. Solar Controller

Usually, a solar panel and a rechargeable battery should not be connected directly for continuous operation. When connecting a solar panel to a battery, it is highly recommended to use a solar charge controller (also known as a solar regulator). Here's why.

Regulated Charging: A solar charge controller regulates the voltage and current coming from the solar panels to the batteries. It ensures that the batteries are charged at their optimal voltage and helps prevent overcharging.

14

Battery Protection: Without a charge controller, there is a risk of overcharging, which can damage the batteries, reduce their lifespan, or even cause them to swell or leak.

Discharge Protection: Many solar charge controllers also prevent the batteries from discharging back into the solar panels at night, which can also cause damage.

Efficiency: Some controllers come with maximum power point tracking (MPPT), which optimizes the charging efficiency, especially in low light conditions. Without a solar charge controller, you risk damaging your battery due to overcharging or deep discharge, and you might not get the best performance out of your solar setup. Therefore, for the longevity of your battery and the overall efficiency of your solar system, using a charge controller is strongly advisable.

An electric current is like the flow of water, which goes from a high level (voltage) to a low level (voltage). To charge a 12 V battery, the output from a solar panel must be slightly higher than 12 V. The solar controller serves as a stabilizer of voltage going from the solar panel to the rechargeable battery. It also serves as a one-way energy controller: during the day when the Sun is bright and high, it prevents the battery from being overcharged by controlling the voltage to be at 12 V at all times, while at night, it prevents the battery from flowing backward to the solar panel to unintentionally drain the battery. Figure 2-2 shows an example of a 10A/12 V solar controller. The two connections to BATTERY are for the 12 V rechargeable lead acid battery. The two connections to LOAD go to either the device (e.g., Arduino UNO board, to be discussed later) or a 12 V to 9 V or 12 V to 7.5 V step-down voltage converter (or transformer; see next section) in our case. The step-down voltage converter is a device which reduces the voltage from 12 V to a lower one (between 7 and 9 V, depending on the type of converter used).

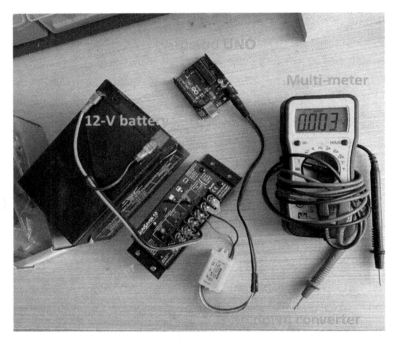

Figure 2-2. *A 12 V to 7 V step-down voltage converter connected to a solar controller and Arduino board*

2.6. Step-Down Converter or Transformer

The internal operational voltage of an Arduino UNO board (which is one of the Arduino boards, to be discussed more later) is 5 V (https://www.arduino.cc/), which can be directly supplied through a USB cable if a stable 5 V DC source is available. A laptop computer usually has at least one USB port which can be used to provide both the 5 V power and connection with the computer for uploading Arduino's computational codes to drive the Arduino board through the Arduino IDE (to be discussed later). Alternatively, the power can be provided through a different external source via a jack connector on the board as the input voltage which is then reduced onboard by Arduino UNO to 5 V DC for operation. The recommended such input voltage is 7-12 V, and this range

16

can be stretched to 6-20 V. A continuous operation of Arduino UNO at an input voltage too much higher than 5 V would cause excessive heat on the Arduino board when the board lowers the input voltage down to 5 V. The higher the difference between the input voltage and 5 V, the more heat it would produce. Because of this, we usually limit the input voltage to be lower than 12 V, especially if we desire to run the Arduino over an extended length of time (e.g., for months or longer). Although Arduino UNO may still work at a voltage of up to 20 V according to its specification, I would not recommend using an input voltage higher than 12 V, especially for long-term deployment, to prevent overheating of the board and damaging of the electronic circuits on the board. Note that the new Arduino UNO R4, however, allows a maximum voltage of 24 V.

To lower the input voltage for an Arduino board to be less than 12 V from the battery, we can use a step-down voltage converter. A step-down voltage converter or step-down transformer is a device that converts a given DC voltage to a lower DC voltage. It is sometimes called a step-down DC-DC converter. It is a very useful component allowing us to lower the input voltage to the Arduino board, thereby reducing the chance of overheating the Arduino board itself. A DC-DC converter usually has an input end and an output end. Each end has a positive and a negative connection. The lower center of Figure 2-2 shows an example of a 12 V to 7 V step-down DC-DC converter connected to a solar controller and Arduino UNO board.

2.7. Battery Enclosure and Desiccant

For continuous operation, particularly with an outdoor deployment, the electronics and battery need to be placed inside a protective enclosure that is weather-resistant (though not necessarily waterproof). This enclosure shields the electronics and battery from the Sun, rain, and moisture to some extent. The enclosure can be plastic or fiberglass but should be rated for outdoor usage to withstand long-term deployment. Figure 2-3 shows an example of a weatherproof plastic enclosure, large enough to house the battery, solar controller, sensors, accessories, Arduino board, and a bag of replaceable silica gel desiccant for moisture control. Silica gel desiccant is important to minimize the negative impact of moisture on electronics. The enclosure is not fully isolated from the outside environment and is not moisture-proof: a small ventilation is needed to measure air pressure correctly if an air pressure sensor is included inside the battery enclosure. For air temperature and humidity, it is not recommended to include them in the battery enclosure. A separate ventilated solar radiation shield enclosure should be used for the air temperature and humidity sensors (see Chapter 9 for more details).

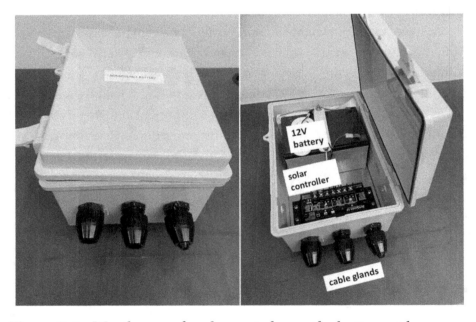

Figure 2-3. *Weatherproof enclosure to house the battery, solar controller, sensors, accessories, and the Arduino board. The cable glands provide a water resistant outlet for the wires and a tube for ventilation. The enclosure is a Style B Plastic Outdoor NEMA Box with Solid Door (dimensions: 11-17/64 inch × 7-15/32 inch × 5-1/2 inch) with a light gray finish*

2.8. Cable Glands

Cable glands (Figure 2-4) are connectors between the inside and outside of the protected enclosure. They provide a protected entry to the enclosure to minimize the intrusion of insects, dust, and splashed water from rain, while allowing wires to connect the Arduino board, battery, and sensors inside the box with the solar panel and external sensors (if any) outside. The three black cable glands in Figure 2-3 are used to provide water-resistant outlets for the wires connecting the solar panel and a tube for ventilation to equalize air pressure between the inside and outside of the box for the air pressure sensor. The third cable gland can provide an outlet for wires to be connected to additional sensors (such as a humidity/temperature sensor or an analog or digital anemometer). Readers can also choose to use just two cable glands if no extra external sensors are used. One can also choose to use one cable gland to pass multiple wires if the diameter is large enough. To use the cable glands on the enclosure box, circular holes need to be drilled on the box. This can be accomplished by using a hole saw or a circular cutter, as shown in Figure 2-5.

Figure 2-4. *A cable gland*

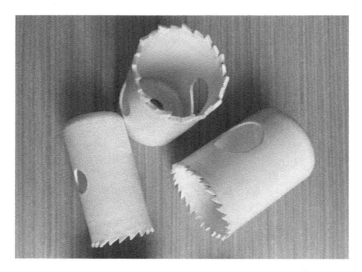

Figure 2-5. *Hole cutters for the cable gland*

2.9. Ventilation Tube

It is recommended that one of the cable glands be used to install a small-diameter tube for ventilation to equalize the air pressure between the enclosure and the outside air. Any small diameter (about a few millimeters) and durable plastic or metal tube can be used. The tube should be inserted into one of the cable glands. If a cable gland is not used, one can drill a small hole for the tube to go through and use glue to seal the edge of the hole. The tube should have enough length (e.g., six inches) to prevent rainwater from entering the enclosure.

2.10. Assembly

There is no need to use a soldering gun to connect the solar controller with the solar panel, solar controller with the battery, and solar controller with the DC-DC step-down converter. All that is needed is a wire stripper (Figure 2-6) and a screwdriver. To connect the DC-DC step-down converter to the power input of Arduino UNO board, however, we will need to connect the output end of the converter to a 2.1 mm pigtail male power plug (Figure 2-7). We can solder the wires together and use a heat-shrink tube (Figure 2-8) to wrap the connection point for better insulation. The pigtail male power plug goes to the Arduino UNO's external power input. At the solar panel end, to connect the solar panel to the battery, use the screwdriver, while at the other end, we can use wire nuts or spade connectors (Figure 2-9) for the connection without soldering and without using heat-shrink tubes.

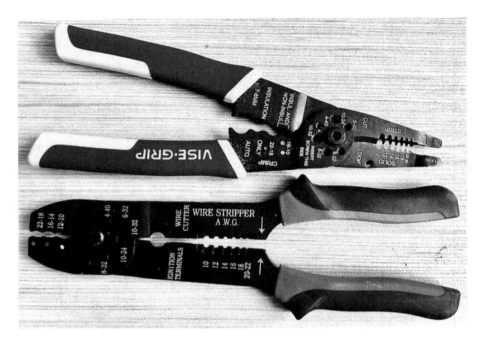

Figure 2-6. *Wire strippers*

When the solar panel, solar controller, battery, DC-DC step-down voltage converter, and Arduino board are connected, they should look like Figure 2-10. Here, the enclosure is omitted – it should contain everything except the solar panel. Omitted here are the sensors connected to the Arduino board, which will be discussed later. The wires used for the connections with the solar panel, battery, and other components should be able to handle the electric current of all the devices or sensors involved, usually not more than a few amps. For example, an 18-gauge stranded two-connector wire (Figure 2-11) should work well for our projects. The wires in Figure 2-11 have two different colors, one for the negative and the other for the positive connections. Always try to stick with this rule (one color for positive and another for negative – in this case, red is for positive and black for negative), as it will be less likely to make mistakes.

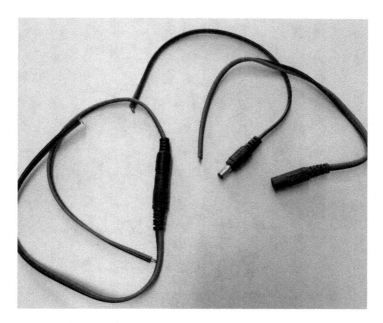

Figure 2-7. *Male and female 2.1 mm pigtail DC power plugs*

Figure 2-8. *Heat-shrink tubes*

Figure 2-9. *Spade connectors (female)*

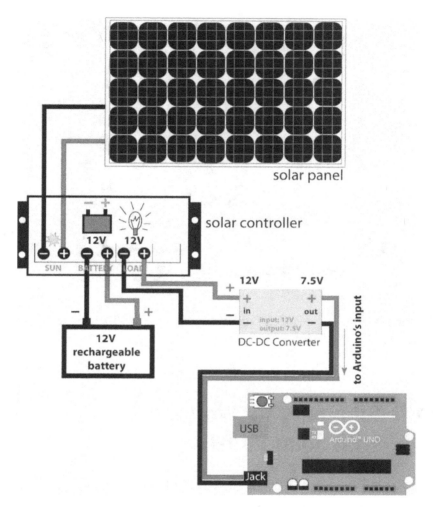

Figure 2-10. *This is a schematic diagram for a common setup to use a solar panel to power the Arduino UNO board. Included here are the solar panel (30-40 W), solar controller, 12 V non-spillable lead acid battery, 12 V to 7.5 V DC-DC voltage converter, and Arduino UNO development board (from Li, 2023)*

Figure 2-11. *An example of wires for the connections. Shown here are 18-gauge stranded two-connector wires*

2.11. Summary for Working with Solar Panel

- A fully charged 12 V battery should read around 12.6 to 13.0 V on a multimeter.

- Place the solar panel outside where it can receive sunlight. Connect the positive terminal of the solar panel to the "SOLAR+" terminal of the solar controller and the negative terminal to the "SOLAR–" terminal.

- Connect the battery's positive terminal to the "BATT+" terminal of the solar controller and the negative terminal to the "BATT–" terminal. Be careful not to short-circuit the battery terminals.

- Use a multimeter to measure the voltage at the "LOAD+" and "LOAD–" terminals of the solar controller. The voltage should be stable and around 12 V. This is the voltage that can be supplied to the step-down converter, which eventually powers the Arduino and sensors.

- Connect the "LOAD+" and "LOAD–" terminals to the input terminals of the step-down converter. The output voltage of the converter should match the input voltage requirement of the Arduino (usually 7 V or 9 V).

- Finally, connect the output terminals of the step-down converter to the Arduino.

By following these steps, you can ensure that your load (Arduino weather station, in our case) receives a stable power supply from the solar panel during the day and from the rechargeable battery at night or during periods of low sunlight.

CHAPTER 3

Arduino UNO Board and Software

3.1. Note on This Chapter

In this chapter, we will briefly cover the basic procedures for working with the Arduino board. If you are already familiar with Arduino boards and the Arduino IDE, you can skip this chapter. This chapter does not include a tutorial for the programming language used in the Arduino IDE, which is a version of C++. We do not always explicitly explain the detailed syntax of the programming language, assuming the user already has basic knowledge. For those with some background in computer coding, learning through example codes should be manageable. There are many books and online resources covering the details (some of them can be found in the "References" section at the end of this book). This chapter is intended as a quick overview and not a complete guide. Users new to the subject may want to consult additional sources for more detailed tutorials. Specifically, this chapter includes basic information about the Arduino IDE, procedures to install an Arduino IDE library, select the correct Arduino board, and select the port the Arduino board is using for communication between the computer and the board. We will then go over some examples from the

© Chunyan Li 2024
C. LI, *Record Weather Data with Arduino and Solar Power*, Maker Innovations Series,
https://doi.org/10.1007/979-8-8688-0814-2_3

Arduino IDE to get started with simple applications, preparing for later chapters involving more in-depth work with the LCD, GPS, SD card, and air temperature, humidity, and pressure sensors.

3.2. Tools and Components

The basic tools and components needed in this chapter are given in Table 3-1. Since this chapter is only aimed at working with the Arduino UNO board with simple testing sketches, there is very little requirement on the tools and components.

Table 3-1. *Components and tools used in this chapter*

Item	Description
Laptop or desktop computer	For uploading and testing computer code for the Arduino
Arduino UNO development board	Development board for working with sensors, GPS, and data logger
USB cable	Connect the Arduino with the computer for uploading and testing computer code for the Arduino board
An LED (optional)	To test an example code
A 220-ohm resistor (optional)	To test an example code

3.3. Arduino UNO Board

The Arduino UNO development board is a popular open-source hardware platform for electronic projects. It belongs to the Arduino family of various development boards that started in 2005. The most popular Arduino UNO board in the last decade (Arduino UNO Revision 3 or R3) includes an 8-bit

AVR microcontroller (ATmega328P) and various components, including voltage regulators for 5 V and 3.3 V, a DC power jack for connecting with recommended external power between 7 and 12 V, a reset button, a USB connector for 5 V power input and communication with a computer for uploading code based on C++, and USB converters, all integrated on a rectangular board of about 6.8 cm × 5.2 cm. Since Arduino boards are open-source, many Arduino UNO compatible boards are produced by various companies. However, this book will only discuss the original Arduino UNO board. With minimal modifications, the projects presented in this book can be adapted to other Arduino boards.

Arduino boards are not computers, but they share some features. For example, they have a central processing unit (CPU) on the microcontroller, which has 32 K flash memory, 2 K static random access memory (SRAM), and 1 K EEPROM memory. Unlike computers, Arduino boards do not have an operating system. Instead, they are often referred to as "microcontrollers." While based on microcontrollers, Arduino boards include additional components for electronic projects.

The Arduino UNO now has a new release, R4, which includes the Arduino UNO R4 Minima and Arduino UNO R4 WiFi. These new boards are based on the 32-bit Arm Cortex-M4 microcontrollers and have 16 times more memory. They use the same 5 V operating voltage and are compatible with the UNO R3, meaning the wiring and codes used for R3 should also work on R4 boards.

3.4. Arduino IDE Software

The software for coding Arduino boards is the Arduino integrated development environment (Arduino IDE), available for free at Arduino Software (https://www.arduino.cc/en/software). The software package can be used on Windows, macOS, or Linux. Downloading and installing the software is straightforward. New users should spend some time learning how to use this software. There are books and online resources available.

The Arduino IDE uses a language similar to C and C++. Arduino programs, sometimes called sketches, must be uploaded onto the Arduino board before executing the tasks intended by the instructions in the sketch.

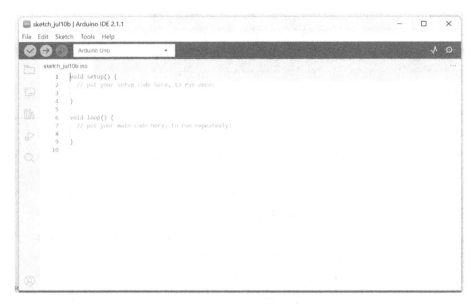

Figure 3-1. *Arduino IDE window*

After installing the Arduino IDE, starting the software will show a default window similar to Figure 3-1, which displays the basic structure of an Arduino program with a setup section and a loop section. The board is designed to execute instructions repeatedly, hence the loop section. Users unfamiliar with the Arduino IDE should consult introductory materials or online training before proceeding. The official Arduino website, Arduino (https://www.arduino.cc/), provides ample information for the projects discussed in this book. A good way to learn programming in the Arduino IDE is through experimenting with the examples included in the IDE. By clicking "File" and then "Examples" on the IDE, users can access various examples categorized as "Built-in examples," examples associated with the board in use (Arduino UNO in this case), and "Examples from Custom Libraries." For instance, if one is working with a GPS module, the user should first install relevant libraries for the GPS module so that not only the GPS module can be used but also the examples within the library are available.

3.5. Arduino IDE Libraries

The Arduino sketches often require the use of libraries, similar to other computer programs. Libraries serve as toolboxes that allow users to apply predefined functions and instructions to their Arduino projects without needing extensive technical skills or reinventing the wheel each time. Without these libraries, programming would be challenging for users who lack professional training in low-level computer programming.

Working with specific sensors typically necessitates relevant libraries, which simplify programming by handling many details of sensor operations, input/output, and interactions within the Arduino board's microcontroller and memory. Some libraries come preinstalled with the Arduino IDE. Occasionally, when a sketch is written or loaded, the IDE will prompt the user to install a required library. The IDE can sometimes detect the need for a library that hasn't been installed yet.

Because the Arduino platform is open-source, many companies and users can contribute new libraries, enriching the available tools. The official Arduino website provides comprehensive information on the IDE's libraries, including tutorials on writing libraries and lists of available ones. These libraries cover various functions such as communications, data processing, data storage, device control, display, memory control, signal input and output, audio control, USB control, and robotics controls. For example, there are over 30 official communication libraries and nearly 900 community-contributed communication libraries, with these numbers continually growing.

Installing an additional library is straightforward. First, download the library, usually a zip file from a specific website like GitHub. Once downloaded, open the Arduino IDE. In the IDE window, select Sketch, then Include Library, and finally Add .ZIP Library (Figure 3-2). This allows the user to browse their computer for the zip file and install it automatically.

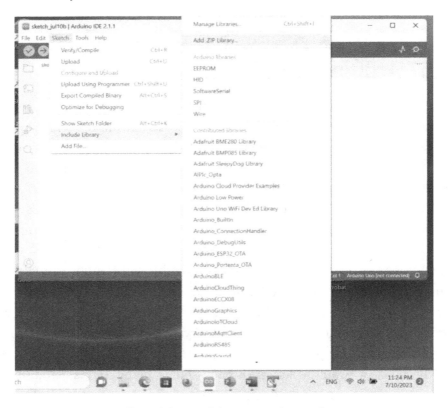

Figure 3-2. *Manually adding a library to the Arduino IDE*

In this book, we will need multiple libraries. It is recommended that the users install the relevant libraries before they start doing anything with the Arduino boards, although they can always wait until they need the library, e.g., the library for running the liquid crystal display (LCD), which is a zip file named "LiquidCrystal-master.zip", and the libraries for running GPS modules, e.g., files named "TinyGPS-13.0.0.zip" and "Adafruit_GPS_Library-1.7.4.zip" (or different versions with slightly different names). Other recommended libraries include "Adafruit-BMP085-Library-master. zip", "Adafruit-BME280-Library-master.zip", "Adafruit-BMP280-Library-master.zip", and "Adafruit-BMP3XX-Library-master.zip".

3.6. About the Power Supply to Arduino

During coding and testing, the Arduino UNO can be powered by a direct link with the computer using a USB A to USB B cable. The USB cable provides a stable 5 V to the board directly. When this USB cable is plugged into the computer, there is no need to supply additional power using the DC power jack of the Arduino. The USB cable provides both power and communication between the Arduino board and the computer. The DC power jack can be used for operation when the USB cable is not plugged in. It is used after the coding is done. Unlike the USB cable, the DC power jack only provides power, but there is no communication function. The power supply through the DC jack should be between 7 and 12 V. This is higher than 5 V because the board will take the power and go through its own filtering to have a smooth and steady 5 V for operation. For the power supply, we can use a 110 VAC to 12 VDC, or 110 VAC to 9 VDC converters available on the market. We can also use alkaline batteries or solar panels. With solar panels, the power from the solar panel should go through a solar controller (see Chapter 2) which typically has an output of 12 VDC. A step-down DC-DC converter is recommended so that the 12 VDC is brought down to around 7.5 VDC to reduce heat dissipation on the Arduino board, thereby prolonging the life of the board as much as possible.

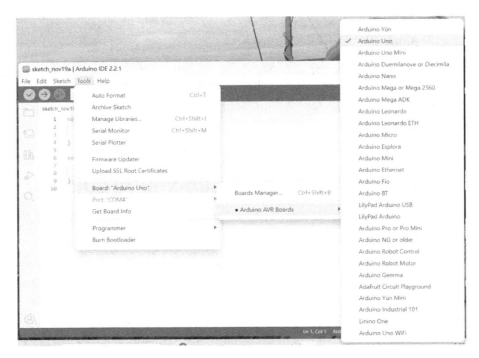

Figure 3-3. *Select the Arduino board in the Arduino IDE*

3.7. Working with the Arduino Board

Plug the USB cable into the Arduino UNO board and computer. Start the
Arduino IDE. Go to "Tools" and select "Board". From the dropdown menu,
select "Arduino Uno" (Figure 3-3) or the board you are using. Also, under
"Tools", select "Port"; from the dropdown menu, select the port (Figure 3-4)
that is connected with your Arduino board (in the example given in
Figure 3-4, the port is COM4). Here, the "Port" is a "serial communication"
port through which data is transferred in sequence via a single wire. This
is apparently a "simple" and commonly used method in computer data
transmission. If you do not see any port available, there may be something
wrong with the connection.

After the board and port are selected correctly, we can use some example sketches in the Arduino IDE to test the Arduino UNO. For instance, in the Arduino IDE, go to "File", select "Examples", and then from the dropdown menu, select "01. Basics" and then select "Blink" (Figure 3-5). This will load the sketch Blink.ino into the Arduino IDE. The sample sketch of the IDE is shown in Figure 3-6. Since the Arduino board has an LED already connected to pin 13 of the board, the user can test the examples below without using the optional LED and 220-ohm resistor (Table 3-1). The blinking of the onboard LED is controlled by the example sketches. Alternatively, the user can connect one of the two legs of the 220-ohm resistor to pin 13 of the Arduino board and the other leg of the resistor to the positive (longer) end of the LED. The negative (shorter) end of the LED is connected to ground (GND) of the board. With this wiring, upload the sample sketch to the Arduino board. This external LED will start to blink. In this case, the blinking of the LED is shown by this external LED.

Figure 3-4. *Select the port in the Arduino IDE*

On the Arduino IDE window, there are three buttons under the main menu. It includes a check mark and a right-pointed arrow. Click the arrow to upload the example sketch into the Arduino UNO board. The compiler of the IDE will first try to compile the code, indicated by the message "compiling sketch ..." at the lower right corner of the IDE window. If there is no error in the sketch, the IDE will first finish "compiling" the code and show a message "Done compiling." The sketch is now converted to digital instructions for the Arduino board and uploaded onto the board indicated by the message "Uploading ...". If successful after a few moments, the IDE will show that the instructions are successfully uploaded by the message "Done uploading." (Figure 3-7).

For this example, after the uploading of the code, one of the LEDs on the Arduino UNO board will blink 1 second after which there is a 1-second delay, and this repeats itself indefinitely until the power is unplugged or until the board stopped working. If you press the reset button on the Arduino board, it will restart the program.

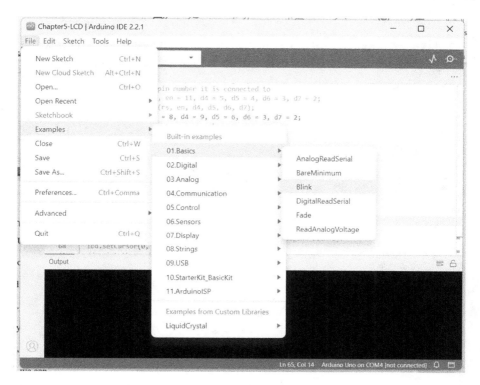

Figure 3-5. *Load an example code "Blink.ino" in the Arduino IDE*

If we examine the code:

```
// the setup function runs once when you press reset or power
the board
void setup() {
  // initialize digital pin LED_BUILTIN as an output.
  pinMode(LED_BUILTIN, OUTPUT);
}

// the loop function runs over and over again forever
void loop() {
  digitalWrite(LED_BUILTIN, HIGH);  // turn the LED on (HIGH is
                                    the voltage level)
```

```
delay(1000);                          // wait for a second
digitalWrite(LED_BUILTIN, LOW);       // turn the LED off by
                                         making the voltage LOW

delay(1000);                          // wait for a second
}
```

Figure 3-6. *An example code "Blink.ino" in the Arduino IDE*

The function pinMode sets the built-in LED to receive digital output (1 to turn on, 0 to turn off). The function digitalWrite(LED_BUILTIN, HIGH) turns the LED on – here, the second parameter in the parentheses HIGH means that the voltage is set at "high" level, typically corresponding to the provided supply voltage (VCC). When the parameter HIGH is replaced by LOW, the voltage becomes 0. In the digital world, HIGH means 1 and LOW means 0. The frequency of blinking and interval of delays can be controlled by the last few lines. The number 1000 within the first delay function or "command"

```
delay(1000);                    // wait for a second
```

is to keep the LED on for 1 second. The number 1000 within the second delay command

```
delay(1000);                    // wait for a second
```

is to keep the LED off for 1 second. Here, the unit of the number is millisecond. These lines lead to the onboard LED to be on and off with the same length in time (1 second). We can change the blinking of the LED by changing these two numbers, for example, if we change these delay commands to the following and upload the code again by clicking the arrow icon on the upper left corner of the IDE:

```
delay(100);                     // wait for a second
digitalWrite(LED_BUILTIN, LOW);   // turn the LED off by
                                  making the voltage LOW
delay(1000);                    // wait for a second
```

We will observe the LED blinking briefly each time with the same delay. The user can experiment and examine different combinations of these delay commands to achieve different effects.

41

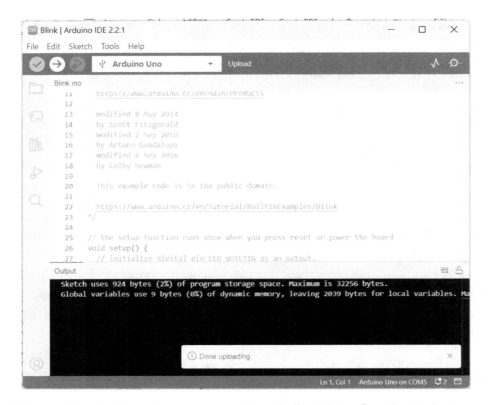

Figure 3-7. *Uploading the example code "Blink.ino" to the Arduino UNO board by pressing the arrow button*

The above example provides a method to undertake certain tasks at given intervals using the delay command. The drawback of this method is that when a delay command is issued, the Arduino is not going to do anything until the delay is finished. There are alternative ways to implement a computational task at intervals without using the delay command. This is given in another example of the IDE, which can be found in "File" ➤ "Examples" ➤ "02.Digital" ➤ "BlinkWithoutDelay". It uses an Arduino IDE's internal function

currentMillis

to return a time variable in milliseconds and compare with a user-defined interval for actions. For more information of this example, one may consult the documentation on the Internet at this web address: `https://www.arduino.cc/en/Tutorial/BuiltInExamples/BlinkWithoutDelay`.

The sketch uses an "if" command to determine when the blinking should be performed or repeated. This avoids asking the Arduino to stop doing things (with a delay command). The delay command puts the processor in hold until the time interval is completed, but the "if" conditional command allows the processor to continue operating and check the conditions to determine the route of the actions of the Arduino.

CHAPTER 4

Working with a GPS Module Without Coding

This chapter introduces basic concepts of the Global Positioning System (GPS) module without the need for coding. It will involve simple wiring between a laptop or an Arduino board and an inexpensive GPS module through a series of hands-on activities or experiments. These activities will help demystify GPS and prepare you for subsequent work with coding in the Arduino IDE.

GPS modules can receive and output GPS data without any coding. Although there are multiple pins on a GPS module, the essential connections include only four wires: positive voltage (usually 5 VDC, though some modules use 3 VDC), ground, TX (data transmission), and RX (data reception). For our applications, more sophisticated controls are unnecessary; receiving GPS data at a default rate of 1 Hz using these four connections is sufficient for our projects.

4.1. Tools and Components

The basic tools, software packages or programs, and components needed in this chapter are listed in Table 4-1.

© Chunyan Li 2024
C. LI, *Record Weather Data with Arduino and Solar Power*, Maker Innovations Series,
https://doi.org/10.1007/979-8-8688-0814-2_4

Table 4-1. *Components and tools used in Chapter 4*

Item	Description
Laptop or desktop computer	For uploading and testing computer code for the Arduino
A GPS module	For work with GPS data (you can use, e.g., a U-Blox GPS module available on Amazon or Adafruit GPS from https://www.adafruit.com/)
FTDI Serial to USB cable	To connect the GPS module with computer for testing
Jump wire/DuPont wire	Colored male-to-female wires to connect the serial end of the "FTDI Serial to USB cable" to the GPS module
Solder station and solder	For soldering the male header onto the GPS module for connection and testing
Break-away type 0.1-inch male header	For the GPS module for connection and testing
Digi's XCTU	A software package for configuring XBee RF modules for data transmission using radio signals (https://www.digi.com/xctu). Here, we use it just for view and save GPS data from the GPS module
Seaterm232	A software package from Sea-Bird Electronics for streaming GPS data from the GPS module to a laptop or desktop computer
U-Center	A software package from U-Blox for easy testing GPS modules
Arduino UNO development board	Development board we use throughout this book for working with sensors and electronic projects
USB B cable for Arduino UNO	Connect the Arduino with the computer for uploading and testing code for the Arduino board

4.2. Some Basic Information

Before we begin working with the GPS module, we will briefly review some basic concepts related to weather data collection. The first concept is time, the second is the Global Positioning System (GPS), and the last is the NMEA sentence. While we do not need to know the technical details of GPS, having a conceptual understanding will help avoid confusion when interpreting the weather data that we will collect using the Arduino board and sensors.

4.2.1. About Time

In your web browser, access the real time for the Eastern Time Zone of the United States using the following address: `https://time.is/ET`. This site will display the date and the current time down to the second. If you want to check the local time, simply use `https://time.is`. For Coordinated Universal Time (UTC), you can use `https://time.is/UTC`, which represents the "world time" or "time for the Earth" (see Figure 4-1).

Figure 4-1. *An example of real time in UTC from the web at*
`https://time.is/UTC`

A general concept of time is based on the idea that "noon is the time when the Sun is at its highest position during the day, and midnight is 12 hours after the previous noon and before the next noon." A day is defined as having 24 hours, with each hour divided into 60 minutes and each minute into 60 seconds. This is called solar time, meaning it is based on the Sun's apparent position in the sky. Since the Earth's surface is a sphere and it rotates, solar time differs at different longitudes.

However, the time we use daily isn't exactly solar time. Raw solar time is inconvenient because (1) adjacent cities at different longitudes would have different solar times and (2) solar time isn't uniform throughout the year, as Earth's elliptical orbit around the Sun causes seasonal variations, among other reasons. These irregularities make solar time unsuitable for scientific measurements.

Historically, people used mean solar time (averaged over a year) and time zones. The Earth is divided into 24 time zones, roughly every 15 degrees of longitude per zone. I say "roughly" because geopolitical factors influence time zone boundaries, so they're not strictly based on longitude. For example, the United States has six time zones: Eastern, Central, Mountain, Pacific, Alaska, and Hawaii, while China, despite spanning five time zones geographically, uses only one time zone: Beijing Time.

The zero longitude, which passes through Greenwich, England, defines the well-known Greenwich Mean Time (GMT). However, GMT has its drawbacks because it is based on solar time, which is irregular. Even mean solar time, though averaged, is still irregular, albeit with smaller errors. To address this irregularity, Coordinated Universal Time (UTC) was proposed and gradually adopted between the 1960s and 1972.

Unlike GMT's top-down approach, where time is defined based on Earth's rotation, UTC uses a bottom-up approach. UTC defines the length of 1 second precisely based on atomic oscillations, with 1 minute as 60 seconds and 1 hour as 60 minutes. The advantage of this method is that the lengths of a second, minute, and hour are accurate and independent of Earth's rotation, unlike GMT. The drawback is that over time, this definition would diverge from the actual length of a day on Earth. This divergence occurs because, besides the irregularity of solar time, Earth's rotation is gradually slowing due to tidal friction, which decreases Earth's angular momentum. As a result, UTC and mean solar time accumulate a slow, dynamic difference. Without correction, after tens of thousands of years, noon UTC would occur in the morning, inconsistent with today's conventions.

To keep UTC consistent with averaged solar time, leap seconds are added when needed, either on June 30 or December 31, to match mean solar time. Since 1972, 27 leap seconds have been added to UTC. However, we don't need to worry about this small variation in everyday life. The key point is that UTC is the current world time, based on atomic time, and it corresponds to the local time at Greenwich, England. Before UTC, GMT was the world time standard. Although people sometimes still refer to GMT, they are usually talking about UTC. World time is also called Z-time, Zero-time, or Zulu time, especially in aviation, weather data, satellite data, and military contexts. Sometimes, the letter "Z" is included in data records to indicate that the time is UTC rather than local time.

Meteorologists typically use UTC to record their measurements. Recording the time and location of environmental data, including weather data, makes sense, as weather forecasts for a region like the contiguous United States require observational data spanning several time zones. A global weather model would cover all 24 time zones, so recording weather data in local time would be impractical. It would be chaotic to analyze weather data from different time zones if each station recorded data in its local time, not to mention the complications of daylight saving time. Therefore, it's standard practice to record weather and oceanographic data in UTC.

Here's an example of seven records (seven lines) of weather data from an Automated Surface Observing System (ASOS) on Barter Island, Alaska:

```
station,valid,lon,lat,tmpc,dwpc,relh,drct,sped,alti,gust_mph
PABA,2022-10-31 12:52,-143.5819,70.1340,-11.11,-13.89,79.93,
130.00,10.35,30.05,M
PABA,2022-10-31 13:18,-143.5819,70.1340,-11.00,-13.00,85.17,
110.00,5.75,30.06,M
PABA,2022-10-31 13:38,-143.5819,70.1340,-11.00,-13.00,85.17,
120.00,5.75,30.06,M
PABA,2022-10-31 13:42,-143.5819,70.1340,-11.00,-13.00,85.17,
110.00,6.90,30.06,M
PABA,2022-10-31 13:49,-143.5819,70.1340,-11.00,-13.00,85.17,
100.00,6.90,30.06,M
PABA,2022-10-31 13:52,-143.5819,70.1340,-10.61,-12.78,84.07,
110.00,6.90,30.06,M
PABA,2022-10-31 13:56,-143.5819,70.1340,-11.00,-13.00,85.17,
120.00,5.75,30.07,M
```

The first line is the header of the data file, which provides brief information about the variables included in the data. In this example, the header indicates that the data includes the station ID (station), date and time (valid), longitude (lon) and latitude (lat) of the station, air temperature in Celsius (tmpc), dew point temperature in Celsius (dwpc), relative humidity (relh) in percentage, wind direction (drct) in degrees, wind speed in miles per hour (sped), air pressure in inches of mercury (alti), and gust wind speed in miles per hour (gust_mph). The four-letter code "PABA" represents the station name, and "2022-10-31 12:52" indicates the year, month, day, hour, and minute in UTC.

The next two numbers in each row, "-143.5819" and "70.1340," are the longitude and latitude of the ASOS station, indicating that the station is located at 143.5819 W, 70.1340 N. These are followed by the values of the other parameters. Unless otherwise specified, the time in standard ASOS weather data is always in UTC.

4.2.2. The NMEA Sentence

Before we work on the GPS module, it's important to understand the concept of an NMEA sentence. NMEA stands for the National Marine Electronics Association. An NMEA sentence is a line of ASCII text data (including decimal numbers) that is reported by an electronic device, such as a GPS, navigational instrument, weather sensor, wave sensor, or another source.

ASCII stands for the American Standard Code for Information Interchange. One advantage of ASCII data is that it can be read by any text reader on a computer and is also readable if printed on paper. This contrasts with binary data, which, if printed on paper, would be incomprehensible. Binary data must be decoded or interpreted by a computer program to be understood.

4.2.3. About Global Positioning System

The Global Positioning System (GPS) is a technology developed by the US government, based on a constellation of at least 24 satellites orbiting the Earth in medium Earth orbit (MEO) at an altitude of about 20,000 km. Each satellite circles the Earth twice a day, continuously transmitting radio signals to receivers on the ground, allowing them to calculate their geographic locations in real time.

GPS receivers, which are widely available on the market, typically include a control panel with a liquid crystal display (LCD), an antenna, and a battery power system. Publicly available GPS receivers can report accurate time and position as frequently as five to ten times per second (5-10 Hz), although the standard output rate is 1 Hz.

At the core of a GPS receiver is the GPS module, an electronic board with minimal components designed to be integrated into systems like cellphones or custom-built GPS units. This module receives signals from GPS satellites and calculates the receiver's three-dimensional position and time. The GPS receiver can output NMEA sentences in ASCII format, showing the position and time at specified intervals.

An example of NMEA sentences reported by a GPS module is shown below.

```
$GPRMC,030123.000,A,3023.0815,N,09103.6838,W,0.10,28.49,
060112,,,A*4D
$GPRMC,030124.000,A,3023.0813,N,09103.6839,W,0.03,357.75,
060112,,,A*7B
$GPRMC,030125.000,A,3023.0814,N,09103.6837,W,0.03,359.36,
060112,,,A*7A
$GPRMC,030126.000,A,3023.0813,N,09103.6837,W,0.03,3.73,
060112,,,A*73
$GPRMC,030127.000,A,3023.0813,N,09103.6836,W,0.04,333.44,
060112,,,A*70
$GPRMC,030128.000,A,3023.0812,N,09103.6835,W,0.03,4.47,
060112,,,A*7E
$GPRMC,030129.000,A,3023.0811,N,09103.6836,W,0.04,356.33,
060112,,,A*7F
```

The dollar sign at the beginning of the sentence indicates that it is an NMEA sentence. The first two characters, "GP," specify that this line contains Global Positioning System (GPS) data. The following characters, "RMC," indicate that this line is the "recommended minimum data for GPS." The interpretation of the sentence is provided below (from left to right).

$GPRMC,hhmmss.ss,A,llll.ll,a,yyyyy.yy,a,x.x,x.x,xxxx,x.x,a*hh

1) hhmmss.ss: Time (UTC)
2) A: Status, A means valid data; V = Navigation
   receiver warning
3) llll.ll: Latitude
4) a: N or S (N is short for north; S is short for south)
5) yyyyy.yy: Longitude
6) a: E or W (E is short for east; W is short for west)
7) x.x: Speed over ground in knots
8) x.x: Course over ground in degrees true
9) xxxx: Date, ddmmyy
10) x.x: Magnetic Variation, degrees E (east) or W (west)
11) a: Mode, A means autonomous; D means DGPS; E means DR (only
    applies to NMEA version 2.3 and later)
12) hh: Checksum

In an NMEA sentence, the checksum is a two-character hexadecimal value located at the end of the sentence, following the asterisk (*) symbol. It is calculated by performing a bitwise XOR operation on all the characters between the $ (start of the sentence) and the * (before the checksum). The resulting checksum value is then appended to the sentence. When the GPS receiver or device receives the sentence, it calculates the checksum in the same way and compares it to the received checksum. If they match, the data is considered valid; if they don't, it indicates potential corruption or error in the transmission. The above discussion covers just one of the options for NMEA sentences in GPS data, specifically the $GPRMC sentence. Additional options are available, as shown in Table 4-2. For example, the first option (GGA) corresponds to GPS data sentences starting with $GPGGA. We will encounter these when we work with our GPS module later in this chapter.

Table 4-2. NMEA output messages (from NMEA Reference Manual)

Option	Description
GGA	Time, position, and fix type data
GLL	Latitude, longitude, UTC time of position fix and status
GSA	GPS receiver operating mode, satellites used in the position solution, and DOP values
GSV	The number of GPS satellites in view satellite ID numbers, elevation, azimuth, and SNR values
MSS	Signal-to-noise ratio, signal strength, frequency, and bit rate from a radio beacon receiver
RMC	Time, date, position, course, and speed data
VTG	Course and speed information relative to the ground
ZDA	PPS timing message (synchronized to PPS)
150	OK to send message

DOP, dilution of precision (related to error propagation); SNR, signal to noise ratio; PPS, pulse per second

4.3. Testing with a GPS Module Using Arduino IDE

Now, let's dive into working with a GPS module using the Arduino IDE. Assuming you have a GPS module, such as the U-Blox GPS module shown in Figure 4-2, you'll typically find four essential connections: VCC (for connecting to the positive terminal of a 5 V DC power source, sometimes a GPS module only requires 3 V DC), GND (for connecting to the ground of the 5 V power source), RX (for receiving signals), and TX (for transmitting signals).

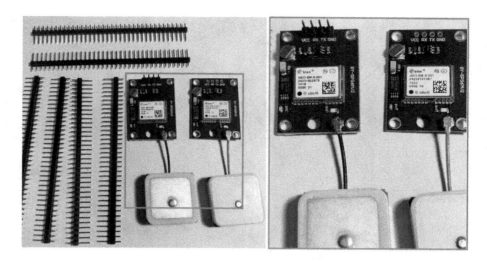

Figure 4-2. *Example of two GPS modules and 0.1" break-away male headers. One GPS module does not have the header soldered into the four connection holes while the other already has the header soldered on the board. The right-hand side is a zoomed-in view of the GPS modules*

Here is a list of a few steps to do the first test on a GPS module.

Step 1. Prepare the Header Pins: Break off four pins from the 0.1-inch break-away male header. Do not break the four pins into individual pins.

Step 2. Solder the Header: Solder the four-pin header to the GPS module. Figure 4-2 shows two identical GPS modules, one with the header soldered on and one without.

Step 3. Connect the GPS Module: Use male-to-female jumper wires to connect the soldered header on the GPS module to the FTDI Serial to USB cable (Figure 4-3). The FTDI cable usually has six colored wires, but only four are needed. Connect the red wire to VCC, black to GND, green to RX, and yellow to TX on the GPS module (Figure 4-4).

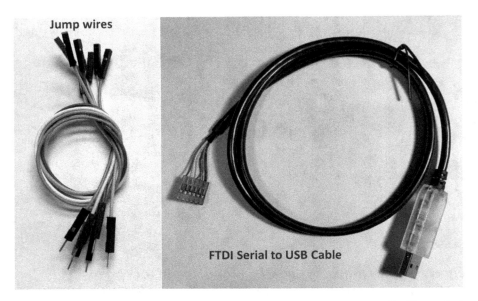

Figure 4-3. *Male-to-female jump wires or DuPont wires (left) and the FTDI Serial to USB cable (right)*

Step 4. Connect to the Computer: Plug the USB end of the FTDI cable into a computer running Windows.

Step 5. Open Arduino IDE: Launch the Arduino IDE (the version I am running is Arduino IDE 2.3.2).

Step 6. Select the Board: In the Arduino IDE menu, click `Tools` which shows a dropdown menu, choose `Board`, and then in the right-hand extension window, choose `Arduino AVR Boards` to display another dropdown list of boards (Figure 4-5). Select any board from the list (e.g., `Arduino UNO`). The specific board doesn't matter for this GPS module test.

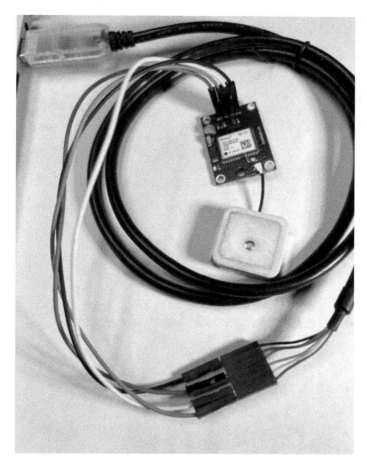

Figure 4-4. *A U-Blox GPS module connected to a laptop computer using the FTDI Serial to USB cable. The green light on the GPS board indicates that it has found a fix*

Figure 4-5. *Choose an Arduino board*

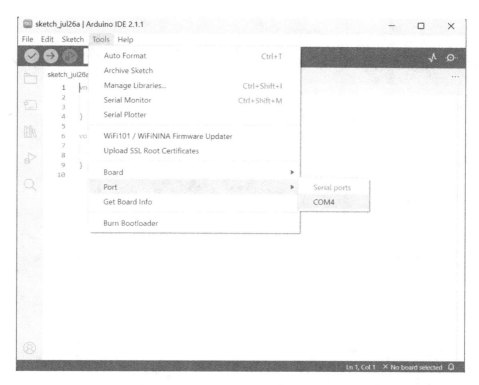

Figure 4-6. *Select the com port to which the GPS module is connected to*

Step 7. Choose the Com Port: Click Tools again on the Arduino menu, select Port, and then on the right, select the com port that is connected to the GPS module (Figure 4-6). If your computer shows more than one com port and you are not sure which one to choose, you can try to unplug the USB end of the FTDI cable connected to the GPS module and check the Port again to find out which com port disappeared from the list. That disappeared com port must be the one connected to the GPS module. You can then replug the USB end and choose that port when the port reappears.

Figure 4-7. *GPS data shown in the Serial Monitor window at the bottom of the Arduino IDE*

Step 8. Open Serial Monitor: Click Tools again on the Arduino menu, and choose Serial Monitor. You should then see GPS data streaming in the Serial Monitor window in the lower half of the Arduino window (Figure 4-7). The GPS data are streaming at 1 Hz frequency and in the form of NMEA sentences. Note that it takes a few moments before the GPS finds a fix, when the latitude and longitude are determined unless you are testing the GPS module in a concrete or large building in which GPS signals are significantly shielded by the building. Note that a GPS 'fix' refers to the process of the GPS receiver determining its precise location by triangulating signals from multiple satellites. For a GPS receiver to get a 'fix,' it typically needs signals from at least four satellites. Once this is achieved, the GPS can calculate the receiver's latitude, longitude, altitude, and sometimes other information like speed and time. A 'fix' indicates that the GPS has enough satellite signals to provide a reliable position. If a GPS hasn't found a fix, it means it either hasn't connected to enough satellites or is unable to determine its position due to poor signal reception. It is recommended that the test is done where the GPS signal is receivable (e.g., outside any tall building, or in a wooden or brick residential house away from tall buildings). If you are testing it in a concrete or metal building, you will most likely not have a GPS fix. Sometimes, it may take a while for the GPS module to find a fix even if you are in a place away from tall buildings. It should be noted that sometimes the labels on a GPS device or GPS module for the TX and RX are misinterpreted. This is because an RX (TX) of the GPS module is connected to the TX (RX) of the device (such as a computer) for display or computing. You can call it the RX of the GPS module or TX of the device (such as a computer). So, if your GPS module does not get a fix for a long time (such as in 15 minutes) and the connection seems to be fine, you may want to swap the TX and RX lines connected to Arduino. This may sometimes fix the problem if it is caused by incorrect labeling or misinterpretation. To reiterate, the TX pin of the GPS module should be connected to the RX pin of the computer or microcontroller (or any receiving device), and the RX pin of the GPS module should be connected to the TX pin of the computer or microcontroller. If the GPS module isn't working as expected, double-checking the connections and ensuring the TX/RX lines are correctly wired.

Before finding a fix, the NMEA sentences have blank data, indicated by empty fields between commas (Figure 4-7). Below is an example of a few lines of NMEA sentence displayed in the Serial Monitor window during a test:

```
$GPGSV,3,2,10,12,63,276,27,17,14,106,14,19,29,095,,24,04,
227,*72
```

```
$GPGSV,3,3,10,25,29,311,10,29,04,302,11*78
$GPGLL,3024.69967,N,09110.78837,W,145322.00,A,A*70
$GPRMC,145323.00,A,3024.70023,N,09110.78725,W,1.256,,
260723,,,A*67
$GPVTG,,T,,M,1.256,N,2.327,K,A*27
$GPGGA,145323.00,3024.70023,N,09110.78725,W,1,05,8.49,52.2,
M,-26.8,M,,*5D
$GPGSA,A,3,11,12,05,06,17,,,,,,,,18.61,8.49,16.56*0B
$GPGSV,3,1,10,05,43,197,28,06,33,043,13,09,08,061,,11,64,
347,20*78
$GPGSV,3,2,10,12,63,276,26,17,14,106,12,19,29,095,,24,04,
227,05*70
$GPGSV,3,3,10,25,29,311,08,29,04,302,12*72
$GPGLL,3024.70023,N,09110.78725,W,145323.00,A,A*7C
$GPRMC,145324.00,A,3024.70049,N,09110.78725,W,0.970,,
260723,,,A*62
$GPVTG,,T,,M,0.970,N,1.797,K,A*25
$GPGGA,145324.00,3024.70049,N,09110.78725,W,1,04,4.12,50.7,
M,-26.8,M,,*52
$GPGSA,A,2,11,12,05,06,,,,,,,,,4.24,4.12,1.00*07
$GPGSV,3,1,10,05,43,197,28,06,33,043,10,09,08,061,,11,64,
347,19*71
$GPGSV,3,2,10,12,63,276,26,17,14,106,09,19,29,095,,24,04,
227,06*79
$GPGSV,3,3,10,25,29,311,08,29,04,302,10*70
$GPGLL,3024.70049,N,09110.78725,W,145324.00,A,A*77
$GPRMC,145325.00,A,3024.70077,N,09110.78694,W,0.880,,
260723,,,A*6B
$GPVTG,,T,,M,0.880,N,1.631,K,A*26
$GPGGA,145325.00,3024.70077,N,09110.78694,W,1,05,3.47,50.6,
M,-26.8,M,,*52
```

The interpretation of these NMEA sentences can be found in Table 4-2 and the NMEA Reference Manual (citation can be found at the end of the book). Most of the sentences are not needed. For a general purpose of recording date, time, latitude, and longitude, the GPRMC sentence discussed earlier is sufficient and easy to use. Computer codes can be written to extract these parameters only from the GPRMC sentences while ignoring the rest.

4.4. Testing with a GPS Module Using Digi's XCTU

Although the Serial Monitor of Arduino IDE can be used to test the GPS module, it cannot save the NMEA sentences (or GPS data) without programming with the IDE. We will postpone doing the coding but first explore with the GPS module a little more without writing any code. Here, we will show how to use a different software package to test the GPS module allowing us not only to receive the NMEA sentences from the GPS module but also save the GPS data. One software package that I recommend is the Digi's XCTU. This is a program designed for testing the XBee RF modules for data telemetry using radio signals. But XCTU also has a function that allows us to test the GPS signals and save them into a text file. In the following, we will explore this in a few steps.

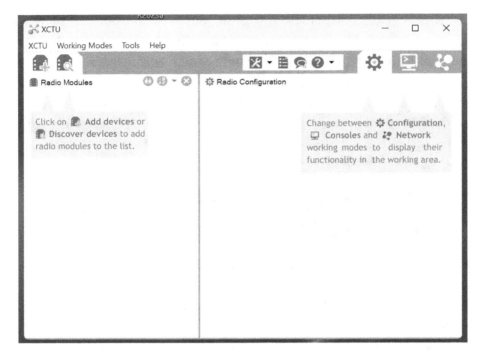

Figure 4-8.   *The window of Digi's XCTU*

Step 1: Download the XCTU program from `https://www.digi.com/xctu`.

Step 2: Install the program on your computer.

Step 3: Start XCTU (Figure 4-8).

Step 4: Plug in the USB end of the FTDI Serial to USB cable, which is connected to the GPS module through the jump wires (DuPont wires) as described earlier.

Step 5: On the upper left corner of the XCTU program window (Figure 4-9), there are two icons of radio modules, one with a plus sign on it (`Add devices`) and the other with a magnifier on it (`Discover devices`). Click the one with a magnifier. A window will pop up with the title `Discover Radio Devices` and **Select the ports to scan** (Figure 4-10). Select the port connected to the GPS module and click `Next >`.

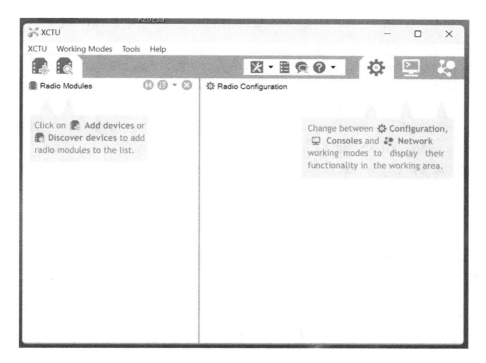

Figure 4-9. *The XCTU window*

Step 6: In the next window, the user can select the parameters for the serial data transmission including the baud rate, data bits, stop bits, and flow control (Figure 4-11). The default should be 9600, 8, 1, and None, respectively, for these parameters. This should work with the U-Blox GPS modules. Some GPS modules might use 4800 baud rate. Press Finish. It will pop up another small window showing 0 device(s) found, unless you have a XBee radio module plugged in. Since we are not working with an XBee radio module here, we can ignore that. Press Close. It will pop up another window titled Radio modules not found and asks Do you want to try with a different configuration? Click No.

Step 7: On the XCTU window, click Tools on the menu and then Serial Console on the subsequent popup window. This leads to another popup titled Serial Console. On the upper left corner, click Open icon (Figure 4-12). This leads to another popup window asking the user to confirm the data transmission parameters and the selected port. Click OK. This will close the last popup and allow the GPS data to flow and to be displayed on the Serial Console at 1 Hz rate.

Step 8: On the Serial Console window, click the camera icon (Figure 4-13) to record the data and specify the location and file name to save. The saved file can be examined after you finish the test and exit the program.

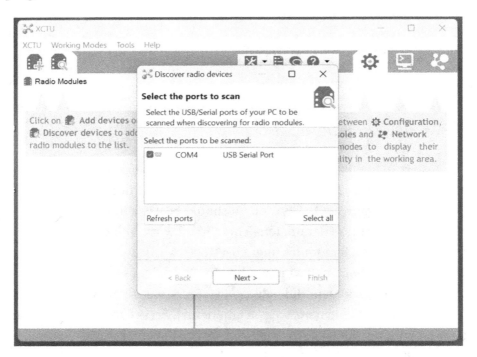

Figure 4-10. *The XCTU window with the popup window after clicking the Add devices, the icon with a XBee radio and a magnifier sign on it. The popup window shows available com ports*

Figure 4-11. *Set the com port parameters in the XCTU program to communicate with the GPS module through the com port*

Figure 4-12. *Preparing to connect with the com port of the GPS module and display the GPS NMEA sentences (GPS data) through the Serial Console*

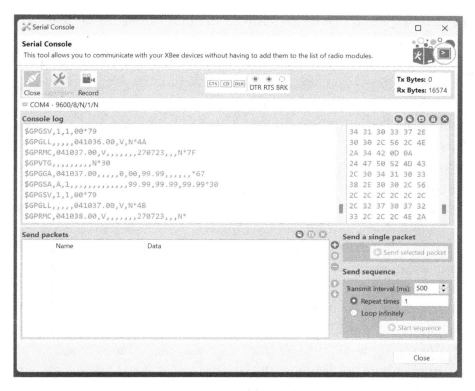

Figure 4-13. *GPS data flowing through the Serial Console in the XCTU program, allowing the user to record the data*

4.5. Testing with a GPS Module Using Seaterm

Another program that can be used to test and record the data from a GPS module is the Seaterm. (If XCTU worked well for you, you can simply skip this section. Seaterm provides a recorded data file by capturing the GPS data going through the Serial Console, in case XCTU does not work for you for some reason.) This is a program of the Sea-Bird Electronics for configuring oceanographic sensors. Although we are not using any of those sensors, the program can serve our purpose testing the GPS modules. The software Seaterm can be downloaded from `https://www.seabird.com/software`. Here, we use Seaterm to do a similar experiment as we have done with the XCTU in the last section. There are multiple ways to do this with Seaterm, depending on which Sea-Bird sensor to choose, but I will just show one way. Note that to use the Serial Console of Seaterm to test the GPS and save GPS data, you do not need to have a Sea-Bird instrument. You just need to pretend you have one of the Sea-Bird Electronics instruments and select one to get to the Serial Console to view and record your GPS data.

Step 1: Download the Seaterm program.

Step 2: Install the Seaterm program on your computer, which should be straightforward.

Step 3: Start Seaterm (Figure 4-14) and plug in the USB end of the FTDI Serial to USB cable which is connected to the GPS module through the jump wires or DuPont wires.

Step 4: On the Seaterm window, click Instruments and choose an instrument from the dropdown list. For example, choose `E. SBE 33 interface`, another Seaterm window titled something like SeaTerm Version 1.59 [SeaTerm] will pop up.

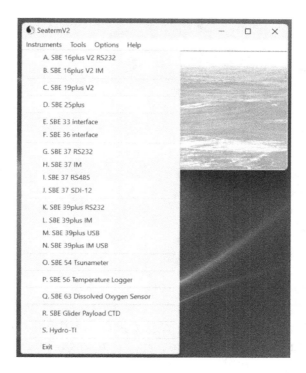

Figure 4-14. *Seaterm program*

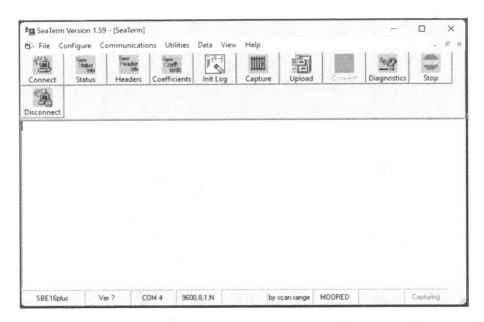

Figure 4-15. *A popup window titled SeaTerm Version 1.59 [SeaTerm] for configuring the comport and for GSP data streaming and recording ("capturing")*

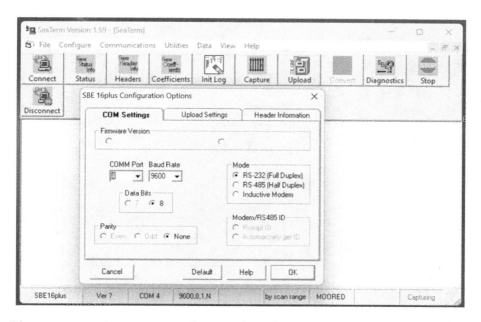

Figure 4-16. *A popup window within the SeaTerm Version 1.59 [SeaTerm] window for configuring the com port*

Step 5: On this popup window, click Configure (Figure 4-15), and then pick any instrument, e.g., SBE 16plus (the user should not worry about what these instruments are because it is irrelevant as far as our purpose of the experiment is concerned). This leads to another popup window (Figure 4-16) titled "SBE 16plus Configuration Options". Here, the user can choose the communication com port parameters. Click OK after the communication port and parameters are selected.

Step 6: Click the upper left most button Connect and watch the stream of NMEA sentences from the GPS module coming through (Figure 4-17)!

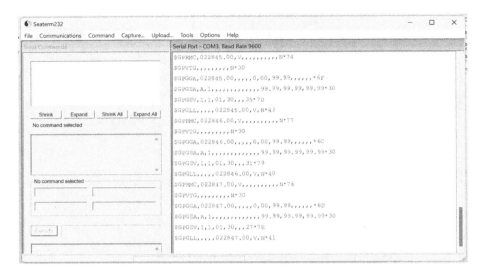

Figure 4-17. *A snapshot of the continuous GPS NMEA sentences streaming on the Seaterm terminal. This snapshot was obtained before the GPS had got a fix*

Step 7: Now we can save the GPS data. While the GPS data is streaming on the console, click the square button named `Capture` on top of the window; the program will prompt the user to provide a file name and folder location to save the GPS data. When you finish the experiment, click the `Capture` button again and the file will be closed though the data is still streaming through the window. Click `Disconnect`; the data will stop coming to the console. The GPS data saved will be in ASCII format in NMEA sentences as discussed earlier (they are just exact copies of the lines of data shown on the screen).

4.6. Testing with a GPS Module Using U-Center

Another alternative software package testing GPS module is the U-Blox's U-Center, which is a software package developed by the U-Blox AG, Switzerland. It can be downloaded from `https://www.u-blox.com/en/product/u-center`. The version that I am using is the U-Center 22.07. The program has a much broader usage than the testing that we are doing here. The users should feel free to explore. In the following, I will just go through a few steps and demonstrate how to use it to test the GPS module and log the GPS data, very much like the previous sections. You may also skip this topic if you have experimented successfully with either XCTU or Seaterm.

Step 1: Download the U-Center program from `https://www.u-blox.com/en/product/u-center` and install the program on your computer or laptop.

Step 2: Plug in the USB end of the FTDI cable connected with the GPS module into your computer.

Step 3: Start U-Center.

Step 4: Click the `Receiver` on the top menu of U-Center. This leads to a dropdown list, check the `Baudrate` (default is 9600, which is good for most GPS modules. Most likely you do not have to change it). If your GPS module's baud rate is different from the checked default value, select the correct one.

Step 5: Still on this dropdown list, click `Connection >` and then choose the com port that is connected to your GPS module (Figure 4-18). Once connected to the GPS module successfully, the U-Center window will display lots of information about the GPS satellites. The program updates the information continuously. For details, consult the U-Center's user guide from their web pages (`https://www.u-blox.com/en/product/u-center`).

Step 6: On the upper left corner, press the red circle to record the GPS data (Figure 4-19).

4.7. Visualization of the GPS Data

The above experiments with XCTU, Seaterm, or U-Center can be done at a fixed location or inside a vehicle driving around where you can use a laptop to save the GPS data of the track. After saving the GPS data, you can visualize the track of the vehicle by using Google Earth. To do that, you need to first convert the GPS file into a format that Google Earth can read, either kml or kmz files. For that purpose, we can use the online GPS Visualizer at `https://www.gpsvisualizer.com/`. This online program allows the user to upload a GPS data file in NMEA sentences (those files saved with the Seaterm, XCTU, or U-Center will all work) and plot the track of the vehicle carrying the GPS module. You can also use this online program to convert the file into kml or kmz format and load the converted file into Google Earth to visualize the track on the Google Earth map. Figure 4-20 is an example of a track from a vehicle carrying a GPS module saved by the XCTU program.

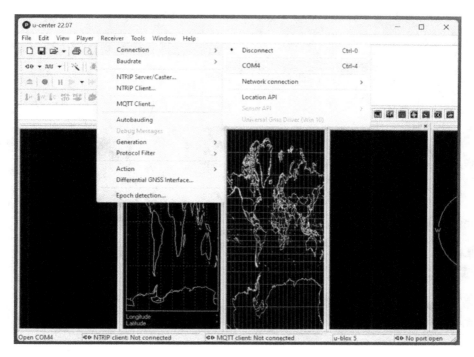

Figure 4-18. *U-Center window. Define the baud rate and select the correct com port connected to the GPS module*

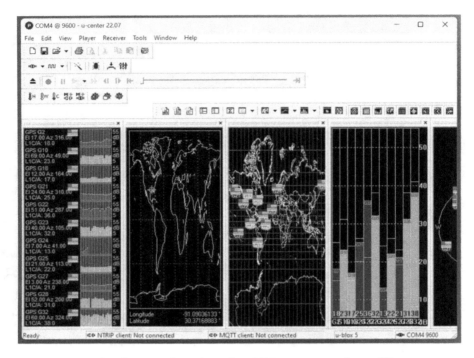

Figure 4-19. *U-Center showing the GPS status and satellite information dynamically*

Figure 4-20. *An example of a vehicle's track using a GPS module and saved by XCTU*

CHAPTER 5

Working with Liquid Crystal Display

5.1. Liquid Crystal Display

Although a display is not required to make an Arduino-based data collection device, it is very useful to be included. It works like a simplified computer monitor which facilitates human–machine interaction and provides the users with feedback and status updates or real-time data as the sensors collect information. For Arduino electronic projects, a commonly used inexpensive display is based on the technology of liquid crystal display or LCD for short. It has a flat glass panel and is lit by a backlight to show pixels that form letters, digits, or even images. What we are going to use are some of the simplest LCDs with two or four rows, although there are more sophisticated versions. They are character LCDs that only print characters (letter, numbers, and ASCII symbols), not images. There are LCDs that can draw images with Arduino boards, but our focus is to have the simplest way to communicate with the Arduino board with relatively straightforward coding. Figure 5-1 is a picture of a mono color 20×4 character HD44780 LCD with 16 connections that require soldering. It can display up to four rows of 20 characters.

© Chunyan Li 2024
C. LI, *Record Weather Data with Arduino and Solar Power*, Maker Innovations Series, https://doi.org/10.1007/979-8-8688-0814-2_5

Figure 5-1. *Picture of a 20×4 character LCD commonly used in Arduino electronic projects. It has 16 connections for power, light intensity control, and data transmission*

Before working with an LCD using the Arduino IDE, the user should make sure that the LCD library is installed in the Arduino IDE. To find out if the library is already installed in the Arduino IDE, go to "File", then "Examples", and check if there is "LiquidCrystal" among the dropdown menu. If not, you need to install this library. The library zip file named "LiquidCrystal-master.zip" can be downloaded from a GitHub web page at `https://github.com/arduino-libraries/LiquidCrystal`. To install the library (as described in general in Chapter 3) in the Arduino IDE, go to "Sketch", then go to "Include Library", then "Add .ZIP library …". This allows you to browse in the computer folders and include the file downloaded from GitHub. The installation takes no time and can be almost instantly finished.

5.2. Tools and Components

The basic tools and components needed in this chapter are listed in Table 5-1. The essential component is the LCD, in addition to the Arduino board. The LCD can be purchased at Adafruit or other online stores. Some of these tools and components can be replaced by similar items. For example, the break-away male headers can be replaced by female headers. This will slightly change the way the connections are made with the LCD, but it does not change the essential wiring diagram.

Table 5-1. *Components and tools used in this chapter*

Item	Description
Laptop or desktop computer	For uploading and testing computer code for the Arduino
Arduino UNO development board	Development board for working with sensors, GPS, and data logger
USB B cable for Arduino UNO	Connect the Arduino with the computer for uploading and testing computer code for the Arduino board
A 16×2 or 20×4 character HD44780 LCD	For use with Arduino board for display of information/ data, monitoring status of the device, or performance of sensors. The 16×2 (20×4) LCD has two (four) rows, each can display 16 (20) characters. Each LCD has 16 connectors that require soldering for making the connections. Such LCDs are available in many stores for Arduino supplies (e.g., Adafruit)
Wire stripper	For wire stripping. It can strip wires of different diameters
Micro-bevel wire cutter	For cutting wires – useful for cutting extra wire soldered on a board
22 AWG (or close in diameter) colored solid wires	Roughly 0.65 mm in diameter. These wires are used as jump wires to connect between the LCD through breadboard and the Arduino UNO board

(continued)

Table 5-1. (*continued*)

Item	Description
Jump wire/DuPont wire	Optional item. Instead of using the colored wires (the 22 AWG wires above), the user can also use jump wire or DuPont wire (see image in Chapter 4, Figure 4-3). Colored male-to-male wires to connect the LCD with the Arduino board. The advantage of using these is that no cutting is needed. The drawback is that they are usually longer than needed
Solder gun	To make connections between the LCD and Arduino, breadboard, adjustable resistor, etc.
Small power strip breadboard	Breadboard for connecting with power (5 V and ground). Two rows with red (+) and blue (−) colors
Breadboard	Breadboard for connecting components such as potentiometer, LCD, and Arduino UNO
1 kΩ or 5 kΩ potentiometer (2)	For work with the LCD for light intensity control
Heat-shrink tubes	For insulation of wires
Heat gun	To work with the heat-shrink tubes
Break-away male-to-male header	For use with the LCD and breadboard for wiring

5.3. Wiring the LCD

To test the LCD, we need to connect the LCD with the Arduino UNO (or compatible) board. Figure 5-2 provides an example for the wiring between the LCD and Arduino. In addition to the Arduino UNO board and LCD, we are also using breadboards (Figure 5-3) for convenience of making the connections. We also use two potentiometers (Figure 5-4) for adjusting the brightness and contrast of the display on the LCD. The diagram in Figure 5-2 represents a standard setup but slightly different from the connections of the "HelloWorld" example under the "LiquidCrystal" on the list of "Examples" of the Arduino IDE. The only difference is the connections to several pins. The modifications are made to make some of the Arduino pins available for the other sensors later in this book.

First, we need to do some soldering to the LCD. There are multiple ways to make electric connections with soldering on the LCD. For example, we can solder one end of each of these wires directly on the LCD (Figure 5-5), and the other end of each of these wires can be connected to the Arduino board, breadboard, and the potentiometers as shown in the wiring diagram (Figure 5-2). We can also solder male-to-male break-away header (see Chapter 4's Figure 4-2) onto the LCD (Figure 5-6); or solder the male end of the male-male DuPont wires to the LCD (Figure 5-7) and use the other male end of the DuPont wires to connect to the breadboard or Arduino pins; or solder the female socket header (Figure 5-8) on the LCD and use wires or DuPont wires to connect to the breadboard and Arduino pins. Note that the pins of socket headers may be 2.54 mm apart while the holes of the 16 connections of the LCD may be 2.50 mm apart. When a ten-pin socket header and a six-pin socket header are used for the 16 connections of LCD, you may need to use a file or sandpaper to remove a thin layer at the edges of headers so they both fit in the holes without too much extra tension. On a HD44780 16×2 or 20×4 LCD, there are a maximum of 16 connections (or pins). Each of the 16 has a name. Without going into the details, one should know their commonly used abbreviated names as shown on the board from pin 1 to 16: VSS, VDD, V0, RS, RW, E, D0, D1, D2, D3, D4, D5, D6, D7, A, and K.

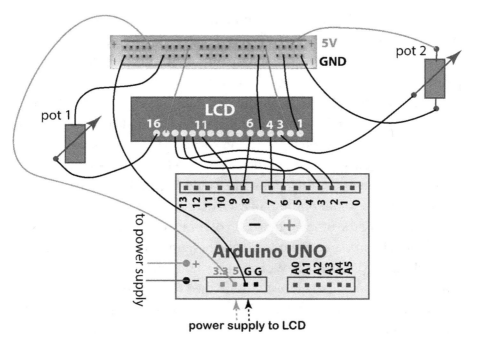

Figure 5-2. *Schematic diagram for wiring the LCD with the Arduino UNO for testing the LCD in this chapter*

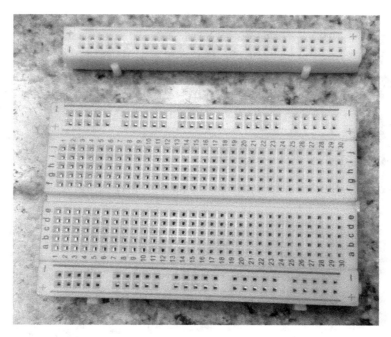

Figure 5-3. *Picture of small power strip breadboard (up) and a breadboard connected with power strips (lower)*

Figure 5-4. *Picture of 4.6 kΩ potentiometers*

Figure 5-5. *Solder colored wires to the LCD directly*

Figure 5-6. *Solder break-away headers to the LCD*

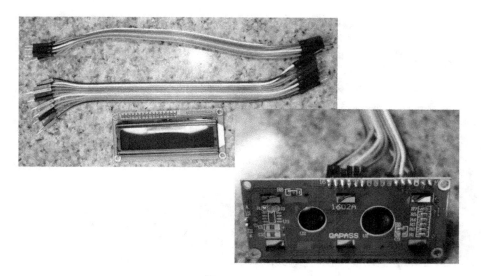

Figure 5-7. *Solder one end of the male-male DuPont wires to the LCD. The other end goes to the sockets on the breadboard or the Arduino UNO board*

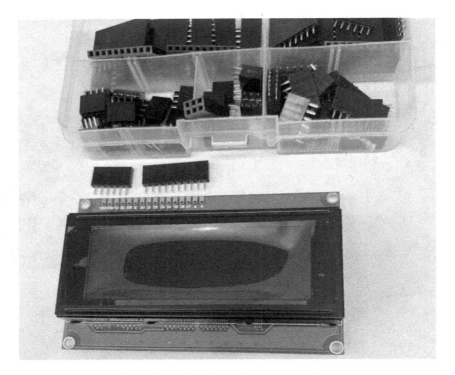

Figure 5-8. *Male-female socket headers as an alternative way to connect the LCD with the Arduino UNO and potentiometers*

After the soldering of the wires on LCD is done, we can now make the connections between the LCD and Arduino UNO board. The diagram of Figure 5-2 should be used for the connections. The LCD has 16 holes (pins) numbered from 1 to 16 for a maximum of 16 connections, but only 12 are used here. Pins 7-10 of the LCD are not connected in this project. On the LCD, only pin 1 and pin 16 are marked. The following is a list of connections to the LCD:

Pin 1 of the LCD is connected to GND (ground).

Pin 2 of the LCD is connected to 5 VDC on the power strip breadboard.

Pin 3 of the LCD is connected to the center line of a potentiometer (POT 2, Figure 5-2).

Pin 4 of the LCD is connected to pin 7 on the Arduino UNO board.

Pin 5 of the LCD is connected to GND.

Pin 6 of the LCD is connected to pin 8 on the Arduino UNO board.

Pins 7-10 of the LCD are left blank.

Pin 11 of the LCD is connected to pin 9 on the Arduino UNO board.

Pin 12 of the LCD is connected to pin 6 on the Arduino UNO board.

Pin 13 of the LCD is connected to pin 3 on the Arduino UNO board.

Pin 14 of the LCD is connected to pin 2 on the Arduino UNO board.

Pin 15 of the LCD is connected to 5 VDC on the power strip breadboard.

Pin 16 of the LCD is connected to the center line of the other potentiometer (POT 1, Figure 5-2).

To supply power to the LCD, a (red) wire is used between the 5 VDC of the Arduino and the 5 VDC (any pin on the red row marked by +) of the power strip breadboard and a (black) wire is used between the GND of the Arduino and the GND (any pin on the blue row marked by –) of the power strip breadboard (as indicated by the arrows at the bottom of Figure 5-2). The use of colored wires is just for convenience of wiring and debugging and for minimizing chances of making mistakes. Of course, the color recommendations are not required – one might choose using only one color throughout or use different color assignment although these are not recommended.

5.4. Testing the LCD

After the wiring of the LCD with the Arduino UNO board is completed, we can now test the LCD using the example codes accessible from the Arduino IDE. Before doing that, the user can now try to power the Arduino UNO board first and adjust the two potentiometers (twist the knobs) to verify changes in brightness and contrast of the LCD, although no characters are shown yet. If the LCD responds to the twist of the knobs with changes in light intensity and contrast, your connections are most likely correct. If the LCD is not lit, or either the intensity or contrast does not change, there must be some problem in the wiring.

After the above verification of the LCD connections, we can now try to run some example code from the Arduino IDE. On the top left of the Arduino IDE, go to "File" and select "Examples" and then select "LiquidCrystal" and then "HelloWorld". This will load the example code (to show the words "hello, world!" on the LCD) into the Arduino IDE in a separate window.

Before modifying any code in the IDE, save the code to your own work directory. From this example script, change the two lines

```
const int rs = 12, en = 11, d4 = 5, d5 = 4, d6 = 3, d7 = 2;
LiquidCrystal lcd(rs, en, d4, d5, d6, d7);
by
```

```
const int RS = 7, E = 8, D4 = 9, D5 = 6, D6 = 3, D7 = 2;
LiquidCrystal lcd(RS, E, D4, D5, D6, D7);
```

Now modify a couple of lines – first, change the line `lcd.print("hello, world!");` to `lcd.print("Display 16x2 LCD");`; second, change the last line `lcd.print(millis() / 1000);` to `lcd.print("Hello, World :)");` just to practice changing code in the IDE environment.

For clarity, if we exclude the comment lines, the code should read:

```
#include <LiquidCrystal.h>
LiquidCrystal lcd(7, 8, 9, 6, 3, 2);

void setup() {
  lcd.begin(16, 2);
  lcd.print("Display 16x2 LCD");
}

void loop() {
  lcd.setCursor(0, 1);
  lcd.print("Hello, World :)");
}
```

After the modification of the code inside the Arduino IDE, you can try to compile the code first and see if any mistakes are introduced. This can be done by pressing the check button on the left-hand side under the main menu in the IDE window. We can then upload it into the Arduino UNO board. To upload the code into the Arduino board, press the arrow button under the main menu of the IDE. The output window of the IDE should show the messages "Uploading..." and "Done compiling ..." (Figure 5-9). These messages are temporary and will disappear in a short moment. You should see the display on the first row of the LCD the words "Display 16×2 LCD". On the second row, it shows "Hello, World :)" (Figure 5-10). With the LCD connected to an Arduino board, one can do many projects with or without additional sensors and components.

5.5. Make a Silent Timer Displayed by an LCD

With the LCD correctly wired, it can be used for interesting projects without using any additional components or sensors. Although it is not necessary that the users do the following experiments, it is a good idea that some practices are done to get familiar with how to code in the Arduino IDE to display numbers and characters or strings of text on LCDs. One of the applications is to make a silent timer displaying time in second and minute from the time of the reset of the Arduino or when the power is plugged in. The following code is an example displaying the time (Figure 5-11), updated every second. To reset or restart, either unplug the power and plug in the power again or press the reset button on the Arduino board.

```
// Saved as Chapter5_LCD_timer5.ino, the result is shown in
Figure 5-11
#include <LiquidCrystal.h> // include the library for the LCD

// THE HD44780 LCD HAS 16 CONNECTIONS, THEY ARE NAMED AS:
//       MAMES   VSS, VDD, VO, RS, RW, E, DO, D1, D2, D3, D4,
D5, D6, D7, A,  K
// LCD PIN NUMBERS  1,  2,   3,  4,  5, 6,  7,  8,  9, 10, 11,
12, 13, 14, 15, 16
// DEFINE THE CONNECTION OF LCD PINS TO THE ARDUINO PINS
const int RS = 7, E = 8, D4 = 9, D5 = 6, D6 = 3, D7 = 2;
LiquidCrystal lcd(RS, E, D4, D5, D6, D7);  // DEFINE THE
                                           LiquidCrystal
                                           AS lcd
                     // ONLY 6 PINS NEED TO BE SPECIFIED
                     // (THE RS, E, D4, D5, D6, D7)
```

```
void setup() {
  // WE ARE USING THE 16X2 LCD
  lcd.begin(16, 2);
  //  lcd.begin(20, 4);  // IF WE USE THE 20X4 LCD
}

void loop() {
    int t; // DEFINE AN INTEGER FOR TIME IN SECOND SINCE THE
              LAST MINUTE
    char min[] = "min"; char sec[] = "sec";
  t = millis() / 1000 - (millis() / 1000/60)*60;
  if (t < 10 ) {  // IF ONE DIGIT FOR THE SECOND SINCE
                    LAST MINUTE
  lcd.setCursor(0, 0); // PUT THE CURSOR AT THE FIRST ROW AND
                          FIRST COLUMN (OR UPPER LEFT CORNER OF
                          THE LCD)
                        // THE ROW OR COLUMN NUMBER STARTS FROM
                          0 IN C OR C++ COMPUTER LANGUAGE
  lcd.print(" "); lcd.print(t); lcd.print(" "); lcd.print(sec);
  lcd.print(" ");
  // PRINT THE TIME IN SECOND
  }
  if (t >= 10) {
  lcd.setCursor(0, 0);
  lcd.print(t);lcd.print(" "); lcd.print(sec); lcd.print(" ");
  // PRINT SECONDS WITH TWO DIGITS
  }
  // THE FOLLOWING PRINTS THE MINUTE SINCE THE RESET OF
  THE ARDUINO
  lcd.print(millis() / 1000/60); lcd.print(" "); lcd.
  print(min); lcd.print("  ");
}
```

The function millis() is an *unsigned long* variable for time in millisecond since the last instance Arduino started running a program. This number will overflow or reset to 0 after about 49 days, although our experiment does not need to last that long but it can if desired. The computation millis() / 1000 gives the time in second, while millis() / 1000/60 gives time in minute. The above code can be modified to the following to display the time in minutes and seconds separated by a column, or in MM:SS format, in which MM is a one- or two-digit number for the minute and SS is a one- or two-digit number for the second (e.g., 5:13 denotes 5 minutes and 13 seconds since one of the following three actions without a power interruption: (1) the upload of the code, (2) reset of the Arduino board, and (3) the power is supplied to the board).

```
// Saved as Chapter5_LCD_timer6.ino, to display time lapsed in
MM:SS format
#include <LiquidCrystal.h>  // include the library for the LCD

// THE HD44780 LCD HAS 16 CONNECTIONS, THEY ARE NAMED AS:
//          MAMES  VSS, VDD, V0, RS, RW,  E, D0, D1, D2, D3,
D4, D5, D6, D7, A,  K
// LCD PIN NUMBERS  1,   2,   3,  4,  5,  6,  7,  8,  9, 10,
11, 12, 13, 14, 15, 16
// DEFINE THE CONNECTION OF LCD PINS TO THE ARDUINO PINS
const int RS = 7, E = 8, D4 = 9, D5 = 6, D6 = 3, D7 = 2;
LiquidCrystal lcd(RS, E, D4, D5, D6, D7);  // DEFINE THE
                                            LiquidCrystal
                                            AS lcd
                        // ONLY 6 PINS NEED TO BE SPECIFIED
                        // (THE RS, E, D4, D5, D6, D7)
void setup() {
  // WE ARE USING THE 16X2 LCD
  lcd.begin(16, 2);
  //  lcd.begin(20, 4);  // IF WE USE THE 20X4 LCD
}
```

```
void loop() {
  // THIS IS CODE FOR A TIMER DISPLAYED BY A 16X2 LCD IN
     MINUTES:SECONDS
  // SINCE THE LAST RESET OF THE ARDUINO
    int t; // DEFINE AN INTEGER FOR TIME IN SECOND SINCE THE
              LAST MINUTE
  t = millis() / 1000 - (millis() / 1000/60)*60;
  lcd.setCursor(0, 0);
  // THE FOLLOWING PRINTS THE TIME IN MINUTE SINCE THE RESET OF
     THE ARDUINO
  // IT IS FOLLOWED BY A COLUMN : AND THEN THE SECOND SINCE THE
     LAST REPORTED MINUTE
  lcd.print(millis() / 1000/60); lcd.print(":");
  if (t < 10 ) {  // IF ONE ONE DIGIT FOR THE SECOND SINCE
                     LAST MINUTE
  lcd.print(" "); lcd.print(t); // PRINT THE TIME IN SECOND
  }
  if (t >= 10) {
  lcd.print(t);  // PRINT SECONDS WITH TWO DIGITS
  }
}
```

With a little more modification, the display can include hours since the latest of the above three actions. The modified code is given below, and the display should look like HH:MM:SS (Figure 5-12). We have added a number to display on the LCD to indicate the hour passed since the latest of the three actions mentioned above.

```
// Saved as Chapter5_LCD_timer7.ino, to display time lapsed in
MM:SS format
#include <LiquidCrystal.h> // include the library for the LCD
```

```
// THE HD44780 LCD HAS 16 CONNECTIONS, THEY ARE NAMED AS:
//          MAMES   VSS, VDD, VO, RS, RW,  E, DO, D1, D2, D3,
D4, D5, D6, D7, A,  K
// LCD PIN NUMBERS  1,    2,   3,  4,  5,  6,  7,  8,  9, 10,
11, 12, 13, 14, 15, 16
// DEFINE THE CONNECTION OF LCD PINS TO THE ARDUINO PINS
const int RS = 7, E = 8, D4 = 9, D5 = 6, D6 = 3, D7 = 2;
LiquidCrystal lcd(RS, E, D4, D5, D6, D7);  // DEFINE THE
                                           LiquidCrystal
                                           AS lcd
                       // ONLY 6 PINS NEED TO BE SPECIFIED
                       // (THE RS, E, D4, D5, D6, D7)
void setup() {
  // WE ARE USING THE 16X2 LCD
  lcd.begin(16, 2);
  //  lcd.begin(20, 4);  // IF WE USE THE 20X4 LCD
}

void loop() {
  // THIS IS CODE FOR A TIMER DISPLAYED BY A 16X2 LCD IN
  hour:MINUTES:SECONDS
  // SINCE THE LAST RESET OF THE ARDUINO
    int t; int t1; // DEFINE AN INTEGER FOR TIME IN SECOND
                   SINCE THE LAST MINUTE
  t = millis() / 1000 - (millis() / 1000/60)*60;
  // SECOND SINCE LAST MINUTE
  t1= millis() / 1000 /60 - (millis() / 1000/60/60)*60;
  // MINUTE SINCE LAST HOUR
  lcd.setCursor(0, 0);
  // THE FOLLOWING PRINTS THE MINUTE SINCE THE RESET OF
     THE ARDUINO
  // IT IS FOLLOWED BY A COLUMN : AND THEN THE SECOND SINCE THE
     LAST REPORTED MINUTE
```

```
lcd.print(millis() / 1000/60/60); lcd.print(":"); lcd.
print(t1); lcd.print(":");
  if (t < 10 ) {  // IF ONE ONE DIGIT FOR THE SECOND SINCE
                          LAST MINUTE
  lcd.print("0"); lcd.print(t); lcd.print(" ");// PRINT
                                            THE TIME
                                            IN SECOND

  }
  if (t >= 10) {
  lcd.print(t); lcd.print(" "); // PRINT SECONDS WITH
                                    TWO DIGITS

  }
}
```

It should be noted that if you are using a 20×4 LCD, in the setup section of the Arduino code, you should use

```
lcd.begin(20, 4);
```

instead of

```
lcd.begin(16, 2);
```

Figure 5-9. *Modifying the example code and uploading the code to the Arduino UNO board*

Figure 5-10. *Display of message from the modified example code*

Figure 5-11. An Arduino UNO-based timer displayed by a 16×2 LCD

Figure 5-12. *Display of the time in HH:MM:SS format*

CHAPTER 6

Saving the Data: Working with SD Card

6.1. SD Card or Micro-SD Card

Saving data to a memory card is often required if the data needs to be analyzed later. With Arduino boards, this is done by using the breakout boards of SD or micro-SD cards. The SD cards have been on the market for more than 20 years and are still commonly used, including the Arduino-based projects. In this chapter, we will go over some simple setup and wiring for the purpose of writing data files on the memory card for later usage.

For our projects, a small capacity memory card is usually more than sufficient. Typically, a card with 0.5 to 8 GB memory will work well. The two kinds of cards (SD or micro-SD) are similar in function with the same wiring requirements, except the difference in size. They may have slightly different designs, such as different power requirements – some use 3.3 VDC, some just use 5 VDC, and some include both 3.3 VDC and 5 VDC. The Arduino UNO board provides both 3.3 VDC and 5 VDC, and they have enough current (power) to support the need of a breakout board of the SD or micro-SD card. Some breakout boards have two GND while others have just one GND. The SD card breakout board or micro-SD card

© Chunyan Li 2024
C. LI, *Record Weather Data with Arduino and Solar Power*, Maker Innovations Series,
https://doi.org/10.1007/979-8-8688-0814-2_6

breakout board (Figure 6-1) we are using can be found in many online vendors such as Adafruit. These breakout boards may or may not have the break-away header already soldered on the board. If an SD or micro-SD card breakout has been included with a break-away header soldered on the board, it can be connected to the Arduino board by either using a breadboard or a female-male DuPont wire. Otherwise, you must solder wires or a break-away header to the board before experimenting with data writing on SD or micro-SD memory card for the projects we do in this chapter.

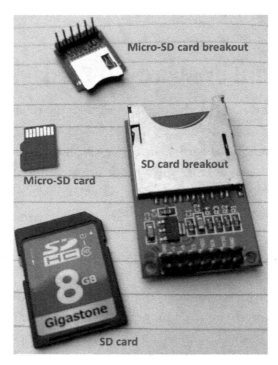

Figure 6-1. *SD card, micro-SD card, breakout board for SD card, and breakout board for micro-SD card*

6.2. Tools and Components

The basic components and tools needed in this chapter are listed in Table 6-1.

Table 6-1. *Components and tools used in Chapter 6*

Item	Description
Laptop or desktop computer	For uploading and testing computer code for the Arduino
Arduino UNO development board	Development board for working with sensors, GPS, and data logger
USB B cable for Arduino UNO	Connect the Arduino with the computer for uploading and testing computer code for the Arduino board
(Micro) SD card breakout board	For use with a SD card to store data
SD card shield	An optional item to replace the SD card breakout board, avoiding some soldering, and do additional experiment
0.5-8 GB (micro) SD card	For use to store data (for cards greater than 8 GB may still work but not recommended here as it is an overkill for our projects)
Wire stripper	For wire stripping. It can strip wires of different diameters
Micro-bevel wire cutter	For cutting wires – useful for cutting the extra wire soldered on a board

(continued)

Table 6-1. (*continued*)

Item	Description
22 AWG (or close in diameter) colored solid wires	Roughly 0.65 mm in diameter. These wires are used as jump wires to connect between the LCD through breadboard and the Arduino UNO board
Jump wire/DuPont wire	Optional item. Instead of using the colored wires (the 22 AWG wires above), the user can also use jump wire or DuPont wire (see image in Chapter 4, Figure 4-3). Colored male-to-male wires to connect the LCD with the Arduino board. The advantage of using these is that no cutting is needed. The drawback is that they are usually longer than needed
Solder gun	To make connections between the LCD and Arduino, breadboard, and adjustable resistor (potentiometer)
Small power strip breadboard	Breadboard for connecting with power (5 V and ground). Two rows with red (+) and blue (–) colors
Breadboard	Breadboard for connecting between components such as potentiometer, LCD, and Arduino UNO
Break-away male-to-male header	For use with the LCD and breadboard for wiring
Small CdS resistor	A sensor that can be used to measure the light intensity
10 kΩ, ¼ W resistor	Used with the CdS resistor as a simple example of sensors
Small toggle switch	Used for turning on and off the writing of data to the SD or micro-SD card

6.3. Wiring the SD Card Breakout Board

To work with the SD or micro-SD memory card on an Arduino board, we need to connect the SD or micro-SD card breakout board to the Arduino UNO (or compatible) board. Figure 6-2 provides a schematic diagram for the wiring between the breakout board and Arduino UNO. In addition to the Arduino UNO board and the breakout board, we are also using a power strip breadboard for convenience of making the connections.

Like the work with LCD in the previous chapter, here we may need to solder a break-away header on the micro-SD or SD card breakout. After the soldering is done, we can then make the connections between the breakout board and Arduino UNO board. The diagram in Figure 6-2 should be used for the connections. Typically, the breakout board has at least six pins or holes. They should include VCC (5 VDC or 3.3 VDC), GND (ground), CS (Chip Select), SCK or CLK (Serial Clock), MOSI (Master Out Slave In, or the Synchronous Peripheral Interface, or SPI, input), and MISO (Master In Slave Out, or the SPI output). The SPI is a synchronous serial communication protocol used in electronics. It is based on a synchronized clock signal shared through a communication bus. The connections should be done as the following:

> The VCC of the breakout board is connected to the VCC on Arduino (or the power strip breadboard, either 5 VDC or 3.3 VDC, depending on which one the breakout is using).

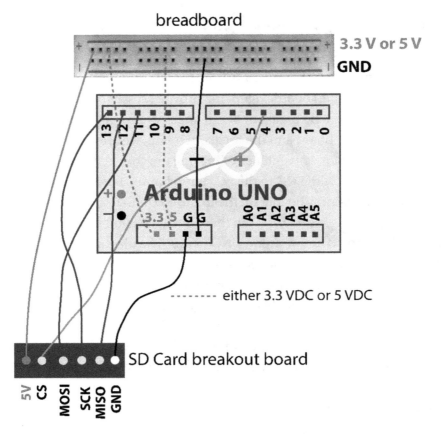

Figure 6-2. *Diagram for wiring the SD card breakout board with the Arduino UNO board*

The GND of the breakout board is connected to GND on Arduino (or the power strip breadboard).

The CS of the breakout board is connected to pin 4 on the Arduino UNO board.

The MOSI of the breakout board is connected to pin 11 on the Arduino UNO board.

The MISO of the breakout board is connected to pin 12 on the Arduino UNO board.

The SCK (or CLK) of the breakout board is connected to pin 13 on the Arduino UNO board.

To supply power to the breakout board, a (red) wire is used between the 5 or 3.3 VDC (depending on which of the voltages is used by the breakout board) of the Arduino (as indicated by the red dotted lines in Figure 6-2) and the 5 or 3.3 VDC (any hole on the red row marked by +) of the power strip breadboard and a (black) wire is used between the GND of the Arduino and the GND (any pin on the blue row marked by −) of the power strip breadboard. The use of colored wires is just for convenience of wiring and debugging and for minimizing chances of making mistakes.

Figure 6-3. *A micro-SD card breakout connected with an Arduino UNO for testing*

6.4. Testing the SD Card

After the wiring is done connecting the SD card or micro-SD card breakout board with the Arduino board (Figure 6-3), we can test it with an example code from the Arduino IDE. Before the test, you should make sure to put a SD card or micro-SD card in the card sleeve on the breakout board (Figure 6-4). In the IDE, go to "File" on the main menu, choose "Examples", and then select "SD" from the dropdown menu, and then "CardInfo". Connect the Arduino UNO board to the computer and upload the code to the Arduino board. Then, go to the main menu again and select "Tools" and then click "Serial Monitor", which will show a window for outputting messages. If the wiring is done correctly, you should see the Serial Monitor window displaying something like this (Figure 6-4):

Figure 6-4. *Running an example code (CardInfo.ino) testing the micro-SD card. The window in the lower half is a Serial Monitor allowing output messages showing whether an SD card is detected and if any files are present in the card*

```
Initializing SD card...Wiring is correct and a card is present.

Card type:          SDHC
Clusters:           242304
Blocks x Cluster:   64
Total Blocks:       15507456

Volume type is:     FAT32
Volume size (Kb):   7753728
Volume size (Mb):   7572
Volume size (Gb):   7.39
```

```
Files found on the card (name, date and size in bytes):
SYSTEM~1/        2023-11-24 23:49:10
  WPSETT~1.DAT   2023-11-24 23:49:10 12
  INDEXE~1        2023-11-24 23:49:10 76
DATALOG0.TXT   2023-11-25 00:47:48 17995
DATALOG.TXT    2000-01-01 01:00:00 39
```

If the card has existing files, the Serial Monitor window prints the file information as well. If on the other hand, there is a problem with the wiring or the SD card, an error message will be displayed (Figure 6-5).

```
Initializing SD card...initialization failed. Things to check:
* is a card inserted?
* is your wiring correct?
* did you change the chipSelect pin to match your shield
  or module?
```

Figure 6-5. *Running an example code testing the micro-SD card. When there is a problem, such as a mistake in the wiring, an error message is displayed showing the card initialization failed*

Figure 6-6. *Running another example code (Datalogger.ino) testing the micro-SD card's ability to save data from three analog sensors. The Output window in the lower half is a Serial Monitor allowing output messages showing the data for three sensors continuously*

6.4.1. Running the Second Example Code with Three Analog Sensors

The above example only tests if the wiring with the SD or micro-SD card breakout board is correct and prints out the card information as well as information about any files that already exist on the card. Now we can run

another example from the SD library within the Arduino IDE to save data
to the memory card. It is the "datalogger.ino" for the SD card examples.
It can be loaded from "File" and then "Examples", "SD", and then select
"datalogger". This will load the code named "datalogger.ino" into the
IDE. The example demonstrates the saving of data from three analog
sensors connected to the analog pins of the Arduino (pins A0, A1, and A3).
To test the code, it is not required to connect the analog sensors, however
(the Arduino board will just read the random voltages at the pins for
sensors). The following lines of code in the example reads the analog data
from the three analog pins and combine them in a string named dataString
in a format of three integers separated by commas:

```
for (int analogPin = 0; analogPin < 3; analogPin++) {
  int sensor = analogRead(analogPin);
  dataString += String(sensor);
  if (analogPin < 2) {
    dataString += ",";
  }
```

The above code consists of a "for loop" and an "if" statement block.
If we do not connect the analog pins to any real sensor, the output data
(the three column numbers) will be random and meaningless but only to
demonstrate that the wiring is correct, and everything works.

If successful, the output window (the Serial Monitor) will produce
something like Figure 6-6 with three columns of numbers updated
continuously. If the SD card is working properly, the card will also save the
three-column series on the memory card in a file named DATALOG.TXT.

Note that the three columns of numbers represent the voltage
measured at the three analog pins of Arduino UNO board – the A0, A1,
and A2 pins. If these pins are connected to the signal output pins of analog
sensors, their values give the measurements at a 10-bit resolution. The
Arduino IDE function analogRead(analogPin) reads the value from the
analogPin, in which analogPin is an integer between 0 and 5 for Arduino
UNO and Arduino Zero, representing the A0 through A5 pins. In Arduino

Mini and Arduino Nano, the analog pins are A0 to A7, while A0 to A15 are analog pins in Arduino Mega, Mega2560, and MegaADK. The Arduino boards have a multichannel and 10-bit analog to digital converter. This means that these boards can convert an input voltage between 0 VDC and the operating voltage (either 5 or 3.3 VDC) to $2^{10} = 1024$ integers (i.e., between 0 and 1023). If we divide 5 into 1024 parts, one part would have $5/1024 = 0.0049$, normalized by the range of measurements. This is the resolution of a 10-bit analog to digital converter for a working voltage of 5 VDC. For a 3.3 VDC, this becomes $3.3/1024 = 0.0032$, normalized by the range of measurements.

6.4.2. Change the Code for Two Analog Sensors

If only two sensors are used in the measurements (each sensor's signal output pin is attached to an analog pin of the Arduino board), the above code can be modified to

```
for (int analogPin = 0; analogPin < 2; analogPin++) {
  int sensor = analogRead(analogPin);
  dataString += String(sensor);
  if (analogPin < 1) {
    dataString += ",";
  }
}
```

6.4.3. Change the Code for Six Analog Sensors

If six sensors are used in the measurements for A0 through A5 (each sensor's signal output pin is attached to an analog pin of the Arduino board), the above code can be modified to

```
for (int analogPin = 0; analogPin < 6; analogPin++) {
  int sensor = analogRead(analogPin);
  dataString += String(sensor);
```

```
if (analogPin < 5) {
  dataString += ",";
}
```

The printout on the Serial Monitor or the saved data in the DATALOG.
TXT file would look something like this:

```
192,191,192,191,193,187
191,189,191,190,193,186
194,192,193,193,196,192
201,198,198,198,204,200
200,198,198,196,196,194
195,194,195,193,191,188
190,191,192,189,186,182
 . . . . . .
```

Again, these numbers are meaningful only when the analog pins (A0 through A5 for Arduino UNO) are connected to the signal output pins of the analog sensors.

6.4.4. When the Voltage of the Analog Pin Is at GND

To test if one of these analog pins, say pin A0, is grounded, what values it would show, we connect the analog pin A0 to GND. The resulted printout in the Serial Monitor or data saved on the SD card in a file named DATALOG.TXT will look something like this:

```
0,12,29,41,61,66
0,10,27,38,56,61
0,10,27,38,56,60
0,12,29,40,59,65
0,12,30,42,62,67
 . . . . . .
```

We can see that the first column is all 0's. This makes sense because the voltage at A0 pin is the same as that of GND which is 0 V.

6.4.5. When the Voltage of the Analog Pin Is at VCC

If we connect the 3rd pin, A2, to 5 VDC, the results look something like this:

```
969,960,1023,1010,998,981
965,956,1023,1010,994,986
979,966,1023,1019,1013,1004
992,976,1023,1016,1012,996
980,968,1023,1007,993,981
965,957,1023,1003,975,966
966,958,1023,1011,994,983
976,964,1023,1014,1003,993
980,967,1023,1012,1006,988
977,965,1023,1008,992,985
973,962,1023,1008,994,978
```

. . . . . .

We can see that the 3rd column prints out 1023, representing the maximum number possible for 2^{10} consecutive integers starting from 0. This also makes sense because the 3rd analog pin A2 is at VCC (5 VDC in this case) so it will take the maximum number.

6.5. Using the SD Card Shield

There are existing stackable SD card shield in the market (Figure 6-7) integrating the SD card breakout on a board which can be inserted into the female headers of the Arduino UNO or compatible to save data to an

SD or micro-SD card. The advantage of using an SD card shield is that the wiring has been done on the board and there is no need to solder or use DuPont wire to connect between a breakout board and an Arduino board. The drawback is that the Chip Select (CS) pin is often fixed with a shield: it is either pin 4, 8, or 10, depending on the brand and design of the shield. In the examples we have just gone through, pin 4 is used. In Figure 6-7, a couple of Seeed Studio SD card shields are shown, with one of them connected to an Arduino UNO – the shield is stacked on the Arduino board.

An SD card shield inserted into an Arduino board   A standalone SD card shield

Figure 6-7. *SD card shields: the left one is inserted into an Arduino UNO; the right one is just the shield. Both have dual cards – the SD and micro-SD card slots*

Using an SD card shield is straightforward, but the user should pay attention to the wiring of the Chip Select (CS) pin of the SD card shield. If CS is not connected to pin 4, the example code must be modified accordingly to make it work. For example, if pin 10 is used for CS, the following line should be used:

```
const int chipSelect = 10;
```

The user can find out which pin is used as CS on a SD card shield from the vendor or by testing different ChipSelect values in the code (try a few options, e.g., chipSelect = 4, or chipSelect = 8, or chipSelect = 10).

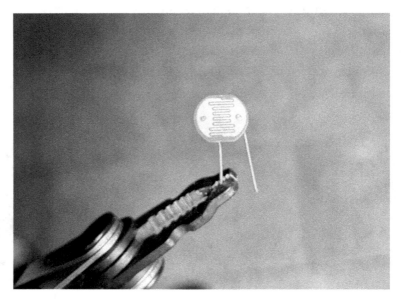

Figure 6-8. *A photocell (CdS photo resistor) which can be used to measure light intensity*

6.5.1. Testing with a Sensor Attached

We can run the example code "datalogger.ino" with one or more analog sensors attached to the analog pins A0 to A5 of the Arduino UNO board. One of the simplest such sensors is a photocell (CdS photo resistor) as shown in Figure 6-8. A CdS sensor can be used to detect light intensity with integer values between 0 (complete darkness) and 1023 ("very bright light"). To include the CdS resistor for this purpose, connect one of the two legs of the CdS resistor to VCC (5 VDC) and the other to an analog pin of the Arduino board, e.g., A0. Then connect a 10 kΩ resistor to GND and the same analog pin, i.e., A0, in this case (Figure 6-9). Figure 6-10 gives the schematic diagram of the connections. We can then run the modified example code for six analog sensors using the SD card shield. Although this sketch can allow up to six sensors, here we only use one sensor to make it simple.

Figure 6-9. *A photocell sensor is attached to the analog pin A0 to record light intensity change over time. A 10 k Ω resistor is also used*

To demonstrate that the sensor works, we can run the code and open the Serial Monitor of the Arduino IDE when there is light in the room where the test is being done. The first column of the printout would have a relatively large value. Since we do not have any sensor connected to the other five analog pins (A1 through A5), the values printed out in the second to sixth columns are not meaningful measurements. The printout in the Serial Monitor window should look something like this:

```
868,666,524,436,347,193, t: 1 sec
868,750,635,543,432,247, t: 2 sec
868,776,685,601,490,319, t: 3 sec
868,785,709,635,532,377, t: 4 sec
868,788,720,654,562,423, t: 5 sec
868,788,723,663,581,462, t: 6 sec
...
```

Now try to gently cover the CdS resistor by your hand, the light intensity is reduced, and the printout will show reduced values in the first column in the Serial Monitor window (also in the DATALOG.TXT file if you check the data later):

```
95,159,205,233,275,167, t: 1056 sec
91,155,202,231,268,156, t: 1057 sec
91,154,202,232,268,164, t: 1058 sec
174,202,231,247,265,145, t: 1059 sec
......
```

If we use a flashlight to shine on the CdS resistor, the first column should have numbers close to 1023:

```
1018,812,661,549,473,533, t: 2 sec
1018,874,746,633,523,667, t: 3 sec
1022,910,799,694,570,658, t: 4 sec
```

```
1014,924,825,734,610,701, t: 5 sec
1021,936,842,758,640,655, t: 6 sec
......
```

The above example is only for a single sensor, but the wiring diagram can be modified to include up to six sensors, with similar connections as shown in Figure 6-10.

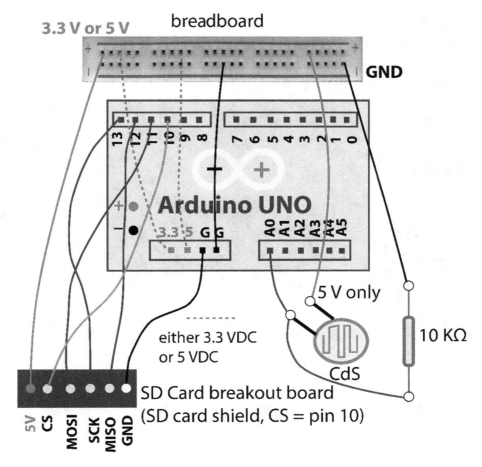

Figure 6-10. *Wiring diagram for the Arduino UNO, SD card breakout board (or shield), a CdS photocell, and a 10 k Ω resistor*

6.5.2. Adding a Toggle Switch As the Sixth Sensor and for Better Control

Now we modify the above example to include a toggle switch as another sensor and to control the time to save the data to the SD card and the time to stop saving data. This is done by connecting the three pins of the switch to an analog pin of the Arduino UNO, e.g., A5, 5 VDC, and GND, respectively (Figure 6-11). The connection diagram is shown in Figure 6-12, a slightly modified version of Figure 6-10.

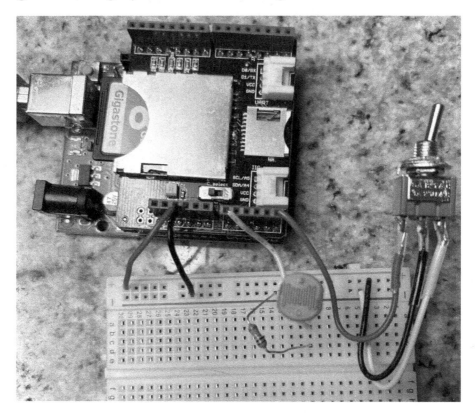

Figure 6-11. *Adding a toggle switch to allow turning on and off the writing of data to the SD or micro-SD card*

We now modify the example code to read the analog signal from A5: when A5 is not grounded, allow the measurements and data writing on the SD card to proceed. This is done by the added codes:

```
int test = analogRead(5);
if (test>0) {}
float t = millis()-(millis()/1000)*1000;
// ~ 0 EVERY 1 SECOND
if (t<=0.0001){ // ~ APPROXIMATELY 0
... ...
}
}
```

The complete code for this modified example is

```
/*
  SD card datalogger

  This example shows how to log data from three analog sensors
  to an SD card using the SD library.

  The circuit:
   analog sensors on analog ins 0, 1, and 2
   SD card attached to SPI bus as follows:
 ** MOSI - pin 11
 ** MISO - pin 12
 ** CLK - pin 13
 ** CS - pin 4 (for MKRZero SD: SDCARD_SS_PIN)

  created   24 Nov 2010
  modified 9 Apr 2012
  by Tom Igoe

  This example code is in the public domain.

*/
```

```
// THIS FILE IS MODIFIED AND NAMED
// Chapter6_Datalogger_CS10_6analogPins_dt_1sec_stop
// - ADDED A WAY TO STOP THE WRITING OF DATA BY GROUNDING
ANALOG 6
// - CL, NOV. 26, 2023

#include <SPI.h>
#include <SD.h>

const int chipSelect = 10; // CONNECT CS OF THE SD-CARD
                           // TO PIN 10 OF ARDUINO UNO
void setup() {
  // GET READY FOR THE SERIAL MONITOR OF THE ARDUINO IDE
  Serial.begin(9600);
  // GET READY FOR THE SD CARD
  Serial.print("GETTING READY FOR THE SD CARD");

  // CHECK IF THE SD CARD IS THERE
  if (!SD.begin(chipSelect)) {
    Serial.println("SD CARD NOT FOUND OR IN ERROR");
  }
  Serial.println("SD CARD IS READY!");
}

void loop() {
  // make a string for assembling the data to log:
  String dataString = "";

  int test = analogRead(5);
  if (test>0) {
  float t = millis()-(millis()/1000)*1000;
  if (t<=0.0001){
  // read six sensors and append to the string:
```

```
for (int analogPin = 0; analogPin < 6; analogPin++) {
  int sensor = analogRead(analogPin);
  dataString += String(sensor);
  if (analogPin < 5) {
    dataString += ",";
  }
}

dataString = dataString + ", t: " + String(millis()/1000)+ "
sec";

// open the file. note that only one file can be open
at a time,
// so you have to close this one before opening another.
File dataFile = SD.open("datalog.txt", FILE_WRITE);

// if the file is available, write to it:
if (dataFile) {
  dataFile.println(dataString);
  dataFile.close();
  // print to the serial port too:
  Serial.println(dataString);
}
// if the file isn't open, pop up an error:
else {
  Serial.println("error opening datalog.txt");
}
}
}
}
```

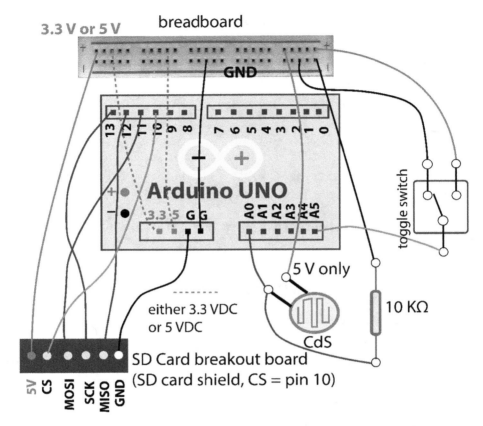

Figure 6-12. *Wiring diagram for the Arduino UNO, SD card breakout board (or shield), a CdS photocell, a 10 k Ω resistor, and a toggle switch*

CHAPTER 7

GPS Recorder

This chapter will discuss more on working with GPS module, and the main difference between this chapter and Chapter 4 is that here we will work with a GPS module through coding. We will start with the simplest coding in which there are no actions taken by Arduino and just allow the GPS data to be streamed through the Arduino IDE's Serial Monitor window. We will then include additional coding to display the GPS data on an LCD, before using an SD card to save the data. We will then add a toggle switch and experiment with a magnetic switch, which will allow us to turn the GPS on and off from outside a waterproof enclosure.

Before working on the coding for GPS module, the user should first make sure that some GPS libraries are installed in the Arduino IDE. These are the TinyGPS and Adafruit's GPS libraries. The TinyGPS can be downloaded from `https://www.arduino.cc/reference/en/libraries/tinygps/`, while the Adafruit's GPS library can be downloaded from `https://www.arduino.cc/reference/en/libraries/adafruit-gps-library/`. Note that the above libraries are just a couple of examples, sufficient for the testing in this book and many applications. There are more GPS libraries which can be found in the official Arduino website, the GitHub, or simply from the Arduino IDE: go to the Sketch on the Arduino IDE, and select Include Library and then Manage Libraries … (or Ctrl+Shift+i). In the "Filter your search" box under LIBRARY MANAGER on the left side of the IDE window, type GPS. It will show a list of libraries related to GPS. You can then choose the desired libraries to install (Figure 7-1).

© Chunyan Li 2024
C. LI, *Record Weather Data with Arduino and Solar Power*, Maker Innovations Series,
https://doi.org/10.1007/979-8-8688-0814-2_7

Figure 7-1. *Installing GPS libraries from the IDE*

7.1. Tools and Components

To work with the GPS modules in this chapter, the basic tools and components are listed below in Table 7-1.

Table 7-1. *Components and tools used in Chapter 7*

Item	Description
Laptop or desktop computer	For uploading and testing computer code for the Arduino
Arduino UNO development board	Development board for working with sensors, GPS, and data logger
USB B cable for Arduino UNO	Connect the Arduino with the computer for uploading and testing computer code for the Arduino board
SD card or micro-SD card breakout board	For use with a SD card to store data
SD card shield (optional)	An optional item to replace the SD card breakout board and avoid some soldering
64 MB to 8 GB SD or micro-SD card	For use to store data
A HD44780 16×2 or 20×4 character LCD	For use with Arduino board to display information/data, monitor status of the device. The 16×2 (20×4) LCD has two (four) rows, each can display 16 (20) characters. Each LCD has 16 connectors requiring soldering. Such LCDs are available in many stores for Arduino board related supplies (e.g., Adafruit)
A 2.1 mm DC pigtail male power plug	This plug is to connect the Arduino UNO with the DC power from the output end of the step-down converter
9 V alkaline battery	To power the GPS recorder
9 V battery connector clip	The positive and negative connector with the 9 V alkaline battery
Wire stripper	For wire stripping. It can strip wires of different diameters

(continued)

Table 7-1. (*continued*)

Item	Description
Micro-bevel wire cutter	For cutting wires – useful for cutting the extra wire soldered on a board
22 AWG (or close in diameter) colored solid wires	Roughly 0.65 mm in diameter. These wires are used as jump wires to connect between the LCD through breadboard and the Arduino UNO board
Jump wire/DuPont wire	Optional item. Instead of using the colored wires (the 22 AWG wires above), the user can also use jump wire or DuPont wire (see image in Chapter 4, Figure 4-3). Colored male-to-male wires to connect the LCD with the Arduino board. The advantage of using these is that no cutting is needed. The drawback is that they are usually longer than needed
Solder gun	To make connections from the LCD to Arduino, breadboard, and potentiometer
Small power strip breadboard	Breadboard for connecting with power (5 V and ground). Two rows with red (+) and blue (–) colors
Breadboard	Breadboard for connecting components such as potentiometer, LCD, and Arduino UNO
Break-away male-to-male header	For use with the LCD and breadboard for wiring
Reed switch	An optional item to turn the GPS recorder on and off in a waterproof way without using a mechanical switch
Double pole double throw (DPDT) switch	Optional switch used to disconnect the GPS module, easier for uploading code to Arduino board when GPS module is connected to pins 0 and 1 of the board
Enclosure box	To hold all components including the Arduino board, SD card, and GPS module, so that the device can be easily transported or deployed for testing and applications

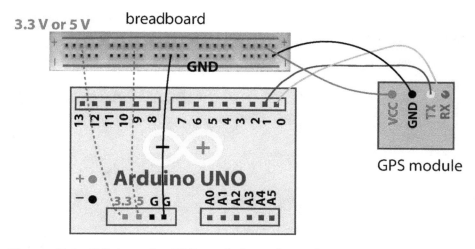

Figure 7-2. *Wiring of a GPS module to the Arduino UNO*

7.2. The Simplest Code for GPS

In Chapter 4, we used a FTDI cable connected to the GPS module and streamed the GPS data to the Arduino IDE's Serial Monitor window without any coding. Now, we will start with coding, but our first test will use just an "empty" sketch, compile, upload the empty program, and see the GPS data streaming into the Serial Monitor window without using the FTDI cable. Let us wire the GPS as shown in Figure 7-2: RX goes to pin 0 of the Arduino UNO board and TX goes to pin 1. Assuming the GPS module uses 5 V, we can use the 5 V from the Arduino board to connect to the VCC of the GPS module. Some GPS modules use 3.3 V, in which case, the 3.3 V on the Arduino board should be used instead. However, in this case, if you still use 5 V, it should be fine, but there may be a little more heat generated on the GPS module because of the extra energy. Do not forget to connect the GND of the GPS to that of Arduino board. We then type two lines of code in the Arduino IDE:

```
void setup() {}
void loop() {}
```

These two lines of coding really do not incur any specific actions as you can see that there is no commands or functions provided.

Figure 7-3. *The simplest GPS module test code "blank" in the examples for libraries*

These two lines are empty setup and loop sections of the Arduino code. This code can also be found in one of the examples of the Adafruit GPS library (Figure 7-3). On the Arduino IDE, go to "File", then *Examples*, then "Adafruit GPS Library", and select "blank" (Figure 7-4). Make sure the correct port and board are selected (under the *Tools* tab of the IDE). Go to Tools again and select Serial Monitor; you should immediately see that the GPS sentences are streaming through the Serial Monitor window continuously (Figure 7-4). It may take a few moments before the GPS output has the full information of time and location when it finds a fix. The Serial Monitor window should use the 9600 baud rate. This code uses the Arduino UNO's default RX and TX pins (digital pins 0 and 1, respectively). These pins can be redefined with more explicit coding (see the next example).

Figure 7-4. *An example from the Adafruit GPS library (for convenience, the file name is modified in this chapter: Chapter7_blank.ino)*

7.3. The Second Test Code for GPS

The second test code for GPS can be modified from another example from the TinyGPS library (assuming you have installed this library – if not, please consult Chapter 4 for installation of libraries). This example can be loaded from the IDE: click "File" tab and select "Examples", then "TinyGPS", and select "simple_test". The original code is for a GPS module with 4800 baud rate, but many GPS modules now use 9600 baud rate, in which case the line

```
ss.begin(4800);
```

should be modified to (Figure 7-5)

```
ss.begin(9600);
```

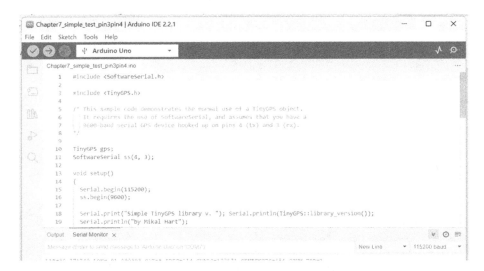

Figure 7-5. *The second code for testing GPS module modified from one of the examples of the TinyGPS library*

Note that sometimes the comments in a sketch or on labels for RX and TX on devices or components might be switched or misinterpreted because RX (reception) and TX (transmission) are all relative to which is the receiver and which is the transmitter. The original comment in this example sketch after the first two #include statements can be used as an example:

```
/* This sample code demonstrates the normal use of a TinyGPS
   object. It requires the use of SoftwareSerial, and assumes
   that you have a 4800-baud serial GPS device hooked up on
   pins 4(rx) and 3(tx).
*/
```

Since the GPS module's TX (RX) is the Arduino board's RX (TX), the connection should be such that the GPS module's TX is connected to pin 4 (not pin 3) and the module's RX is connected to pin 3 (not pin 4). Depending on the viewpoint, the connections might be misinterpreted and the wirings unintentionally swapped.

The baud rate in this example is 115200 so the Serial Monitor window should also use this baud rate – the user needs to manually change it to 115200. Otherwise, the Serial Monitor will not show the results correctly. This number can be modified, but the user just needs to remember to have the same value for the Serial Monitor window.

Here are some sample lines on the Serial Monitor window after finding a GPS fix in the Serial Monitor window:

```
LAT=33.591740 LON=-93.777900 SAT=8 PREC=114 CHARS=133383
SENTENCES=566 CSUM ERR=1
LAT=33.591740 LON=-93.777900 SAT=8 PREC=114 CHARS=133852
SENTENCES=568 CSUM ERR=1
LAT=33.591736 LON=-93.777900 SAT=8 PREC=114 CHARS=134321
SENTENCES=570 CSUM ERR=1

...
```

7.4. Display GPS Data on an LCD

In Chapter 5, we wired an LCD to display text and numbers. Here, we combine an LCD with a GPS module so that we can display information about date, time, and location (longitude and latitude) from the GPS on the LCD rather than on the Serial Monitor of the Arduino IDE. A sample wiring is provided in Figure 7-6. The wiring for the LCD is the same as that in Chapter 5, while the GPS module wiring is the same as Figure 7-2:

Pin 1 of the LCD is connected to GND (ground).

Pin 2 of the LCD is connected to 5 VDC on the power strip breadboard.

Pin 3 of the LCD is connected to the center line of a potentiometer (POT 2, Figure 7-6).

Pin 4 of the LCD is connected to pin 7 on the Arduino UNO board.

Pin 5 of the LCD is connected to GND.

Pin 6 of the LCD is connected to pin 8 on the Arduino UNO board.

Pins 7-10 of the LCD are left blank.

Pin 11 of the LCD is connected to pin 9 on the Arduino UNO board.

Pin 12 of the LCD is connected to pin 6 on the Arduino UNO board.

Pin 13 of the LCD is connected to pin 3 on the Arduino UNO board.

Pin 14 of the LCD is connected to pin 2 on the Arduino UNO board.

Pin 15 of the LCD is connected to 5 VDC on the power strip breadboard.

Pin 16 of the LCD is connected to the center line of the other potentiometer (POT 1, Figure 7-6).

Note that for the GPS module, now RX goes to pin 1 (not pin 0) of the Arduino UNO board and TX goes to pin 0 (not pin 1), opposite of Figure 7-2. Assuming the GPS module uses 5 VDC, we can use the 5 VDC from the Arduino board to connect to the VCC of the GPS module.

The corresponding sketch is shown below:

```
// Chapter7-testUBLOXPGS_TinyGPS_LCD.ino
#include <TinyGPS.h>
#include <LiquidCrystal.h>
// DEFINE THE CONNECTION OF LCD PINS TO THE ARDUINO PINS
const int RS = 7, E = 8, D4 = 9, D5 = 6, D6 = 3, D7 = 2;
LiquidCrystal lcd(RS, E, D4, D5, D6, D7);  // DEFINE THE
LiquidCrystal AS lcd

                        // ONLY 6 PINS NEED TO BE SPECIFIED
                        // (THE RS, E, D4, D5, D6, D7)

TinyGPS gps;

void setup() {
Serial.begin(9600);
  lcd.begin(16, 2); // USE A 16X2 LCD
  lcd.setCursor(0,0); // CURSOR SET AT (0,0) - 1st column
                      & 1st row
  lcd.print("Chapter 7: GPS");
  lcd.setCursor(0,1); // CURSOR SET AT (0,1) - 1st column
                      & 2nd row
  lcd.print("Read GPS ...");
  delay(5000); // delay 5 seconds
}
```

141

```
// A function to get GPS data and print to LCD
void getgps(TinyGPS &gps)
{
  float latitude, longitude; int year;
  byte month,day,hour,minute,second,hundredths;
  gps.f_get_position(&latitude,&longitude);
  gps.crack_datetime(&year,&month,&day,&hour,&minute,&second,
  &hundredths);
  // print GPS data to the LCD
  lcd.setCursor(0,0); lcd.print("Lat: "); lcd.
  print(latitude,5);
  lcd.print("     ");
  lcd.setCursor(0,1); lcd.print("Lon: "); lcd.
  print(longitude,5);
  lcd.print(" ");
  delay(3000); // delay 3 seconds
  lcd.clear();

  lcd.setCursor(0,0); lcd.print("Time:");
  if(hour<10)
  {
  lcd.print("0");
  }
  lcd.print(hour,DEC); lcd.print(":");
  if(minute<10)
  {
  lcd.print("0");
  }
  lcd.print(minute,DEC); lcd.print(":");
  if(second<10)
```

```
  {
  lcd.print("0");
  }
  lcd.print(second,DEC); lcd.print("UTC");

  lcd.setCursor(0,1);
  lcd.print("Date:"); lcd.print(year,DEC); lcd.print(".");
  lcd.print(month,DEC); lcd.print("."); lcd.print(day,DEC);

  delay(3000); // delay 3 seconds
  lcd.clear();

}

void loop() {
  // repeating the following actions:
byte GPSdata;
if (Serial.available() > 0)
{
GPSdata = Serial.read();
 if(gps.encode(GPSdata))
 {
 getgps(gps);
 }
}
}
```

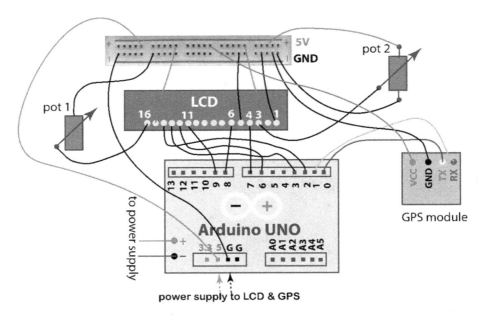

Figure 7-6. *Wiring diagram for testing GPS module with an LCD*

This sketch displays the GPS information on the LCD showing in real time the year, month, day, hour, minute, and second, as well as the latitude and longitude. Figure 7-7 shows a picture of displayed information on LCD using this setup and the code "Chapter7-testUBLOXGPS_TinyGPS_LCD.ino".

Figure 7-7. *Picture showing the Arduino UNO, A NEO-6M (UBLOX 6) GPS module, and a LCD with displayed GPS info using the diagram of Figure 7-6 and using the code "Chapter7-testUBLOXGPS_ TinyGPS_LCD.ino"*

Here, we are connecting the default RX (pin 0) and TX (pin 1) of the Arduino UNO board to the TX and RX of the GPS module, respectively. The drawback of this type of connection is that if the sketch is modified and needs to be uploaded onto the Arduino board again from the computer, the GPS module connected to the Arduino board through these pins may interfere with the uploading process so the new code cannot be uploaded. The TX or RX pins must be disconnected before the upload can be accomplished successfully. If the code is repeatedly modified, the GPS module must be disconnected and reconnected repeatedly, which can be annoying. One remedy is to modify the code and define different TX and RX pins. Alternatively, we can add a double pole double throw (DPDT) toggle switch (Figure 7-8).

Figure 7-8. *Double pole double throw (DPDT) switches*

With a proper coding for the added DPDT switch, when we need to upload a revised code and test it again, we just toggle the switch to the off position before uploading and turn it back on after. A DPDT switch is a switch with two inputs and four outputs; each input has two possible outputs. If this sounds confusing, Figure 7-9 shows the conceptual design. In our case here, we only need to use two of the four output connections. More specifically, the two input connections are connected to the GPS module's TX and RX, respectively (left-hand side of Figure 7-9). The corresponding output connections of these inputs are connected to the Arduino UNO's digital pins 0 and 1, respectively. But pins 3 and 5 of the DPDT in Figure 7-9 are left open (not connected to anything) for our project. When the switch is "on," the input is connected to pins 4 and 6 which go to the Arduino UNO's pins 1 and 0, respectively (right-hand side of Figure 7-9). This makes sure that both pins are connected to the GPS's TX and RX at the same time or disconnected at the same time when the switch is toggled on and off. Some soldering is needed to attach jumper wires on the toggle switch allowing it to make the connections on a breadboard. We only need to "turn off" the GSP when we are trying to upload a revised sketch. After finishing uploading a revised code, we must remember to turn the GPS back on again by using the DPDT switch or there will be no GPS displayed.

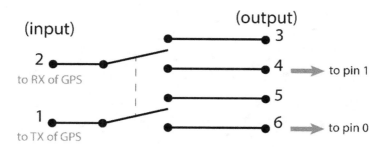

Figure 7-9. *Conceptual diagram of a DPDT switch*

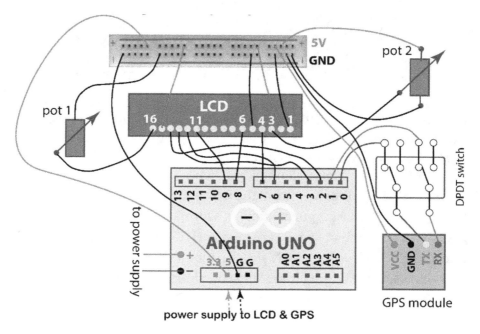

Figure 7-10. *Wiring diagram of Arduino UNO, LCD, and GPS module with a DPDT toggle switch to disconnect and connect the GPS*

147

Figure 7-11. *Picture showing the wiring of the Arduino UNO, A NEO-6M (UBLOX 6) GPS module, an LCD, and a DPDT switch using the diagram of Figure 7-10 and using the code "Chapter7-testUBLOXGPS_TinyGPS_LCD.ino"*

Figure 7-11 shows a picture of the new wiring (compared with Figure 7-7). The GPS output the time in a format of HHMMSS (in this case, 17 hour, 16 minute, and 34 second in UTC) and date (the year 2023, December 17). This screen only stays on momentarily and is switched to another screen showing the latitude and longitude and alternating between these two screens continuously as specified in our sketch below.

7.5. Display GPS Data on an LCD and Save the Data to an SD Card

Now we are ready to move one step further to save the GPS data onto an SD card. By integrating the SD card wiring we discussed in Chapter 6, the LCD wiring in Chapter 5, and the GPS wiring here, we can come up with an integrated design as shown in Figure 7-12.

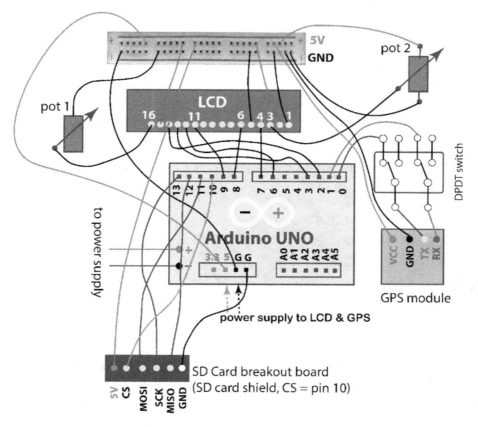

Figure 7-12. *Diagram of wiring for saving GPS data in a SD card and display with an LCD, using the code "Chapter7_GPS_LCD_SDCard.ino"*

As in Chapter 6, the VCC of the SD card breakout board is connected to the VCC on Arduino (or the power strip breadboard, either 5 V or 3.3 V.

The GND of the breakout board is connected to the GND on Arduino (or the power strip breadboard).

The CS of the breakout board is connected to pin 10 on the Arduino UNO board. The user should always double-check which pin is used for CS. Some of the examples use pin 4 for CS. Always check the definition of CS in the code, e.g.,

```
const int chipSelect = 10;
```

means that the CS is pin 10 in this case.

The MOSI of the breakout board is connected to pin 11 on the Arduino UNO board.

The MISO of the breakout board is connected to pin 12 on the Arduino UNO board.

The SCK (or CLK) of the breakout board is connected to pin 13 on the Arduino UNO board.

```
// Chapter7_GPS_LCD_SDCard.ino
#include <TinyGPS.h>
#include <LiquidCrystal.h>
#include <SD.h>
const int chipSelect = 10;
// DEFINE THE CONNECTION OF LCD PINS TO THE ARDUINO PINS
const int RS = 7, E = 8, D4 = 9, D5 = 6, D6 = 3, D7 = 2;
LiquidCrystal lcd(RS, E, D4, D5, D6, D7);  // DEFINE THE
LiquidCrystal AS lcd
                        // ONLY 6 PINS NEED TO BE SPECIFIED
                        // (THE RS, E, D4, D5, D6, D7)

TinyGPS gps; // DEFINE THE NAME OF GPS
```

```
void setup() {
Serial.begin(9600);
  lcd.begin(16, 2); // DEFINE THE DIMENSION OF LCD
  lcd.setCursor(0,0); // PUT CURSOR AT ORIGIN
  lcd.print("Getting ready..."); // PRINT A MESSAGE
  delay(3000); // delay 3 seconds

  if (!SD.begin(chipSelect)) {
  lcd.setCursor(0,1);
    lcd.print("Card failed    "); // PRINT A MESSAGE
      return;
  }
  lcd.setCursor(0,1); // PUT CURSOR AT 2ND ROW
  lcd.println("card OK...       "); // PRINT A MESSAGE
  delay(3000); // delay 3 seconds
  File dataFile = SD.open("GPSData.txt", FILE_WRITE);
  // OPEN DATA FILE TO WRITE
                                              // TO SD CARD
    dataFile.println("NaN, NaN, NaN, NaN, NaN, NaN, NaN, NaN");
// PRINT A LINE
      // THE ABOVE LINE IS INSERTED INTO THE DATA FILE EVERY
         TIME THE
      // ARDUINO IS RESTARTED. THIS WILL MAKE IT CONVENIENT
         TO READ IN
      // MATLAB TO AVOID PROBLEM WITH PLOTTING THE DATA WITH
         LARGE GAPS.
    dataFile.close();
}
```

```
// A FUNCTION TO BE USED REPEATEDLY TO GET GPS DATA
void getgps(TinyGPS &gps)
{
  File dataFile = SD.open("GPSData.txt", FILE_WRITE);
// OPEN DATA FILE TO WRITE
                                            // TO SD CARD
  // DEFINE THE DATA TYPES AND NAMES
  float latitude, longitude; int year;
  byte month,day,hour,minute,second,hundredths;
  // GET THE DATA FROM GPS
  gps.f_get_position(&latitude,&longitude);
  gps.crack_datetime(&year,&month,&day,&hour,&minute,&second,&h
  undredths);
  // PRINT THE LAT & LON ON THE LCD
  lcd.setCursor(0,0); lcd.print("Lat: "); lcd.print(latitude,5);
  lcd.print("     ");
  lcd.setCursor(0,1); lcd.print("Lon: "); lcd.print(longitude,5);
  lcd.print(" "); delay(3000); lcd.clear();
  // PRINT TIME ON THE LCD
  lcd.setCursor(0,0); lcd.print("Time:");
  if(hour<10)
  {
  lcd.print("0");
  }
  lcd.print(hour,DEC); lcd.print(":");
  if(minute<10)
  {
  lcd.print("0");
  }
  lcd.print(minute,DEC); lcd.print(":");
```

```
  if(second<10)
  {
  lcd.print("0");
  }
  lcd.print(second,DEC); lcd.print("UTC");
  // PRINT THE DATE ON THE LCD
  lcd.setCursor(0,1); lcd.print("Date:"); lcd.print(year,DEC);
  lcd.print("."); lcd.print(month,DEC); lcd.print(".");
  lcd.print(day,DEC);
  delay(3000);
  // SAVE THE GPS DATA ON THE SD CARD
    dataFile.print(year,DEC); dataFile.print(", ");
    dataFile.print(month,DEC); dataFile.print(", ");
    dataFile.print(day,DEC); dataFile.print(", ");
    dataFile.print(hour,DEC); dataFile.print(", ");
    dataFile.print(minute,DEC); dataFile.print(", ");
    dataFile.print(second,DEC); dataFile.print(", ");
    dataFile.print(latitude,5); dataFile.print(", ");
    dataFile.print(longitude,5); dataFile.println(" ");
    dataFile.close();
  lcd.clear();
}

void loop() {
  // REPEATEDLY DO THE FOLLOWING TO GET THE GPS DATA,
  // DISPLAY ON THE LCD, AND SAVE ON THE SD CARD
byte GPSData;
if (Serial.available() > 0)
{
```

```
GPSData = Serial.read();
 if(gps.encode(GPSData))
 {
 getgps(gps);
 }
}
}
```

Figure 7-13. *Picture of wiring with Arduino UNO, LCD, SD card breakout, and a DPDT switch*

Note that the DPDT switch is optional and only useful when testing and reloading the sketch. After the codes are finalized, there is no need to have this DPDT switch. It is included here for convenience of testing.

7.6. Adding a Switch

We can now add a switch the same way as in Chapter 6. We can either use a single pole double throw (SPDT) or a single pole single throw (SPST) switch. Figure 7-14 uses the former (a SPDT switch). For a SPST switch, the connection to the VCC is absent. Both should work. The use of the SPDT switch guarantees that, when turned on, the voltage at A5 would be 5 V or the analog reading of A5 is 1023. We add a line in the loop() section of the Arduino code to test if the analog pin 5 (or A5) of the Arduino UNO is connected to GND or not:

```
int test = analogRead(5); // IF A5 PIN IS CONNECTED TO
                          // GROUND, DO NOT READ GPS DATA,
                          OTHERWISE
                          // DO, ALLOWING STOP SAVING
                          // DATA TO SD CARD WHEN THE SWITCH
                          // IS TURNED ON.
```

If A5 is grounded, the voltage is 0. Otherwise, it should be greater than 0, when the commands within the if block will be executed:

```
if (test>0) {
  ...
}
```

155

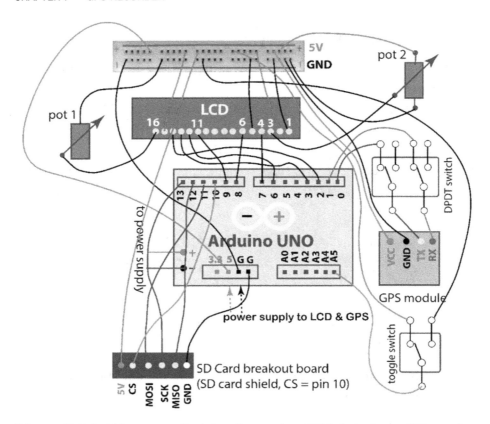

Figure 7-14. *Diagram of wiring for saving GPS data in an SD card and display with an LCD, using the code "Chapter7_GPS_LCD_SDCard_AnalogSwitch.ino" and an SPDT switch*

The complete sketch is provided below for convenience.

```
// Chapter7_GPS_LCD_SDCard_AnalogSwitch.ino
#include <TinyGPS.h>
#include <LiquidCrystal.h>
#include <SD.h>
const int chipSelect = 10;
// DEFINE THE CONNECTION OF LCD PINS TO THE ARDUINO PINS
const int RS = 7, E = 8, D4 = 9, D5 = 6, D6 = 3, D7 = 2;
```

```
LiquidCrystal lcd(RS, E, D4, D5, D6, D7);  // DEFINE THE
LiquidCrystal AS lcd
                        // ONLY 6 PINS NEED TO BE SPECIFIED
                        // (THE RS, E, D4, D5, D6, D7)

TinyGPS gps; // DEFINE THE NAME OF GPS

void setup() {
Serial.begin(9600);
  lcd.begin(16, 2); // DEFINE THE DIMENSION OF LCD
  lcd.setCursor(0,0); // PUT CURSOR AT ORIGIN
  lcd.print("Getting ready..."); // PRINT A MESSAGE
  delay(3000); // delay 3 seconds

  if (!SD.begin(chipSelect)) {
  lcd.setCursor(0,1);
    lcd.print("Card failed    "); // PRINT A MESSAGE
    return;
  }
  lcd.setCursor(0,1); // PUT CURSOR AT 2ND ROW
  lcd.println("card OK...      "); // PRINT A MESSAGE
  delay(3000); // delay 3 seconds
  File dataFile = SD.open("GPSData.txt", FILE_WRITE);
// OPEN DATA FILE TO WRITE
                                              // TO SD CARD
    dataFile.println("NaN, NaN, NaN, NaN, NaN, NaN, NaN, NaN");
// PRINT A LINE
      // THE ABOVE LINE IS INSERTED INTO THE DATA FILE EVERY
      TIME THE
      // ARDUINO IS RESTARTED. THIS WILL MAKE IT CONVENIENT
      TO READ IN
```

```
    // MATLAB TO AVOID PROBLEM WITH PLOTTING THE DATA WITH
    LARGE GAPS.
  dataFile.close();
}

// A FUNCTION TO BE USED REPEATEDLY TO GET GPS DATA
void getgps(TinyGPS &gps)
{
  File dataFile = SD.open("GPSData.txt", FILE_WRITE);
// OPEN DATA FILE TO WRITE
                                              // TO SD CARD
  // DEFINE THE DATA TYPES AND NAMES
  float latitude, longitude; int year;
  byte month,day,hour,minute,second,hundredths;
  // GET THE DATA FROM GPS
  gps.f_get_position(&latitude,&longitude);
  gps.crack_datetime(&year,&month,&day,&hour,&minute,&second,
  &hundredths);
  // PRINT THE LAT & LON ON THE LCD
  lcd.setCursor(0,0); lcd.print("Lat: "); lcd.print(latitude,5);
  lcd.print("    ");
  lcd.setCursor(0,1); lcd.print("Lon: "); lcd.print(longitude,5);
  lcd.print(" "); delay(3000); lcd.clear();
  // PRINT TIME ON THE LCD
  lcd.setCursor(0,0); lcd.print("Time:");
  if(hour<10)
  {
  lcd.print("0");
  }
  lcd.print(hour,DEC); lcd.print(":");
```

```
    if(minute<10)
    {
    lcd.print("0");
    }
    lcd.print(minute,DEC); lcd.print(":");
    if(second<10)
    {
    lcd.print("0");
    }
    lcd.print(second,DEC); lcd.print("UTC");
    // PRINT THE DATE ON THE LCD
    lcd.setCursor(0,1); lcd.print("Date:"); lcd.print(year,DEC);
    lcd.print("."); lcd.print(month,DEC); lcd.print(".");
    lcd.print(day,DEC);
    delay(3000);
    // SAVE THE GPS DATA ON THE SD CARD
       dataFile.print(year,DEC); dataFile.print(", ");
       dataFile.print(month,DEC); dataFile.print(", ");
       dataFile.print(day,DEC); dataFile.print(", ");
       dataFile.print(hour,DEC); dataFile.print(", ");
       dataFile.print(minute,DEC); dataFile.print(", ");
       dataFile.print(second,DEC); dataFile.print(", ");
       dataFile.print(latitude,5); dataFile.print(", ");
       dataFile.print(longitude,5); dataFile.println(" ");
       dataFile.close();
    lcd.clear();
}
void loop() {
    // REPEATEDLY DO THE FOLLOWING TO GET THE GPS DATA,
    // DISPLAY ON THE LCD, AND SAVE ON THE SD CARD
byte GPSData;
```

```
int test = analogRead(5); // IF A5 PIN IS CONNECTED TO
                          // GROUND, DO NOT READ GPS DATA,
                             OTHERWISE
                          // DO, ALLOWING STOP SAVING
                          // DATA TO SD CARD WHEN THE SWITCH
                          // IS TURNED ON.
if (test>0) {
 if (Serial.available() > 0)
  {
    GPSData = Serial.read();
    if(gps.encode(GPSData))
     {
      getgps(gps);
     }
  }
 }
}
```

7.7. Using a Reed Switch

A reed switch is a type of switch operated by a magnetic field. It consists of two ferromagnetic blades sealed within a glass envelope. When a magnet is brought close to the switch, the blades move toward each other, closing the circuit and turning the switch on. Conversely, when the magnet is moved away, the switch turns off.

Figure 7-15 shows several reed switches. A reed switch can replace the SPDT switch connected to the A5 pin of an Arduino UNO to control the writing of GPS data to an SD card using a magnet. This is particularly useful for starting and stopping data recording within a waterproof enclosure without opening it. In this setup, the reed switch is placed inside the enclosure, and a magnet held by the operator can activate the switch through the enclosure. This provides a convenient and safe way to operate a GPS drifter (see section 7.9 below) for recording surface water trajectories, studying wind-driven flows, coastal currents, and the movement of pollutants in the ocean because ocean waters are salty and corrosive, and thus it can easily damage electronics.

Using a reed switch eliminates the need to open the enclosure, which would otherwise expose the electronics to corrosive seawater, potentially damaging the Arduino and GPS module. The code for using a reed switch remains the same as with the SPDT switch. Figure 7-16 shows the wiring diagram using a reed switch, as compared to the SPDT switch in Figure 7-14.

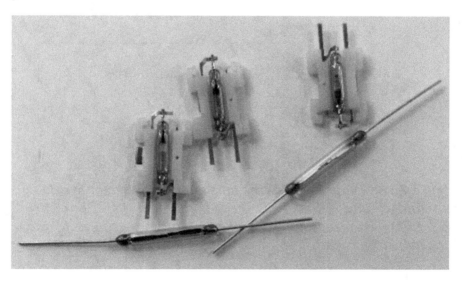

Figure 7-15. *Pictures of some reed switches*

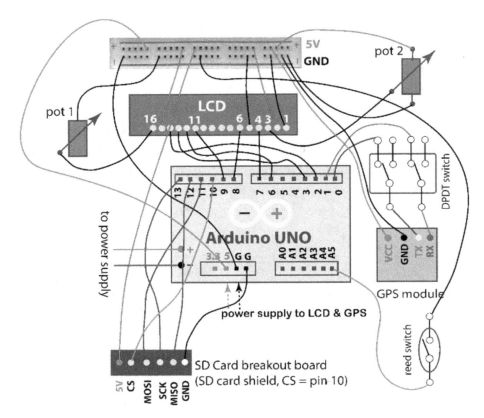

Figure 7-16. *Diagram of wiring for saving GPS data onto an SD card and display with an LCD, using the same sketch "Chapter7_GPS_LCD_SDCard_AnalogSwitch.ino" (given in section 7.6) and a reed switch*

7.8. Using Different Pins for TX and RX

Now let's modify the sketch to avoid using Arduino UNO's pin 0 and pin 1 for TX and RX. In our current design, pins 4 and 5 are still available, so the modified sketch is as follows:

```
// Chapter7-testUBLOXPGS_TinyGPS_LCD_Serial4_5.ino
#include <TinyGPS.h>
#include <LiquidCrystal.h>
#include <SoftwareSerial.h>

// DEFINE THE CONNECTION OF LCD PINS TO THE ARDUINO PINS
const int RS = 7, E = 8, D4 = 9, D5 = 6, D6 = 3, D7 = 2;
LiquidCrystal lcd(RS, E, D4, D5, D6, D7);  // DEFINE THE
LiquidCrystal AS lcd
                        // ONLY 6 PINS NEED TO BE SPECIFIED
                        // (THE RS, E, D4, D5, D6, D7)

// GPS RX connects to Arduino UNO pin 4
// GPS TX connects to Arduino UNO pin 5
SoftwareSerial mySerial(5, 4);

TinyGPS gps;

void setup() {
  lcd.begin(16, 2); // USE A 16X2 LCD
  lcd.setCursor(0,0); // CURSOR SET AT (0,0) - 1st column
  & 1st row
  lcd.print("Chapter 7: GPS");
  lcd.setCursor(0,1); // CURSOR SET AT (0,1) - 1st column
  & 2nd row
  lcd.print("Read GPS .....");
  delay(1000); // delay 5 seconds
}

// A function to get GPS data and print to LCD
void getgps(TinyGPS &gps)
{
  float latitude, longitude; int year; byte month,day,hour,
  minute,second,hundredths;
  gps.f_get_position(&latitude,&longitude);
```

163

```
gps.crack_datetime(&year,&month,&day,&hour,&minute,&second,&h
undredths);
// print GPS data to the LCD
lcd.setCursor(0,0); lcd.print("Lat: "); lcd.
print(latitude,5); lcd.print("     ");
lcd.setCursor(0,1); lcd.print("Lon: "); lcd.
print(longitude,5);lcd.print(" ");
delay(1000); // delay 3 seconds
lcd.clear();

lcd.setCursor(0,0); lcd.print("Time:");
if(hour<10)
{
lcd.print("0");
}
lcd.print(hour,DEC); lcd.print(":");
if(minute<10)
{
lcd.print("0");
}
lcd.print(minute,DEC); lcd.print(":");
if(second<10)
{
lcd.print("0");
}
lcd.print(second,DEC); lcd.print("UTC");

lcd.setCursor(0,1);
lcd.print("Date:"); lcd.print(year,DEC); lcd.print(".");
lcd.print(month,DEC); lcd.print("."); lcd.print(day,DEC);
```

```
  delay(1000); // delay 1 seconds
  lcd.clear();

}

void loop() {
  // repeating the following actions:
  byte GPSdata;
  mySerial.begin(9600);
   if (mySerial.available() > 0)
    {
    GPSdata = mySerial.read();
     if(gps.encode(GPSdata))
      {
        getgps(gps);
      }
    }
}
```

In the sketch, we have added these lines:

```
// GPS RX connects to Arduino UNO pin 4
// GPS TX connects to Arduino UNO pin 5
SoftwareSerial mySerial(5, 4);
```

Since we are not using the default serial TX and RX pins (0 and 1) on the Arduino board, but instead using software-defined communication pins, we have replaced the

```
Serial.available
 by
mySerial.available
```

Specifically, pins 4 and 5 are now used for serial communication between the GPS module and the Arduino. The only wiring change required is to connect the GPS module's RX to Arduino UNO's pin 4 and the GPS module's TX to pin 5.

The advantage of this design is that it eliminates issues with reuploading the sketch after code revisions and removes the need for a DPDT switch.

7.9. Making a GPS Recorder in a Box

In the projects we discussed, it's not necessary to have an enclosure to hold all the electronic components and the Arduino board, especially when we are testing the sketches. However, to create a working product suitable for practical applications, an enclosure is almost essential. For example, if we can fit the Arduino board, GPS module, BME280 (see chapter 8), SD card breakout board, and a battery into a small enclosure with the correct wiring and uploaded sketch, it can be used as a homemade device that can be carried in a backpack while hiking. The SD card can record the track, and the recorded pressure data can be used to demonstrate elevation changes along the route. Additionally, the device could be installed in a car to record topographic changes during a trip, whether in a city or a mountainous region. I've done all of these, and it's a lot of fun, especially when combined with travel, hiking, or even the everyday commute. The data from such a trip can be used in a visualization software package to show the 3-D track.

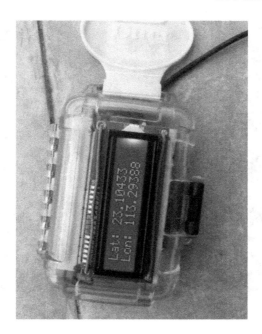

Figure 7-17. *A GPS recorded in a small enclosure*

While most cell phones have built-in GPS, they may not receive a signal in remote areas, which can affect the functionality of the built-in GPS. In contrast, GPS data has global coverage, making a homemade GPS recorder more reliable in such environments. The homemade GPS recorder can easily save data for later analysis. Figure 7-17 shows an example of this GPS recorder in an enclosure. This model includes an LCD, but the LCD is optional. Removing the LCD makes the device lighter and reduces battery consumption, allowing a single battery to last longer. Typically, a new 9 V battery can power the GPS recorder for a few hours. Therefore, if this device is used during a hiking activity to record the 3-D track, it's important to bring replacement batteries.

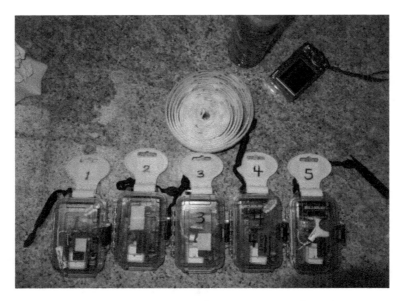

Figure 7-18. *GPS recorders housed in waterproof enclosures, used as drifters to measure ocean surface currents in a student project*

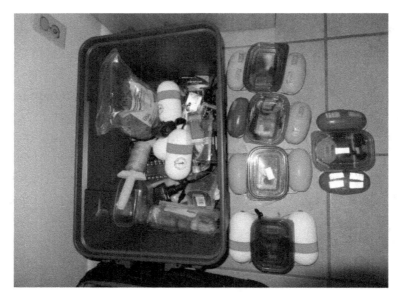

Figure 7-19. *GPS recorders in plastic bags with floats, allowing them to float on surface and drift with the current*

If housed in a waterproof enclosure, the GPS recorder can be used as a surface drifter to estimate ocean surface current velocity. This setup requires additional work to place the enclosure in a carrier with flotation. Deploying and retrieving the drifter(s) also necessitates the use of a small boat. Figure 7-18 shows five GPS recorders in waterproof enclosures. Figure 7-19 shows these GPS recorders in plastic bags with floats, allowing them to drift on the surface with the currents, prepared for a student beach experiment. Magnetic switches were used for easy operation to start and stop the recording of GPS data. Figure 7-20 displays the trajectories of the drifters after the student GPS drift experiment at a Florida beach. Table 7-2 presents some sample results from the drifter experiment, including both the magnitude and direction of surface velocity along the beach, as estimated from the GPS data.

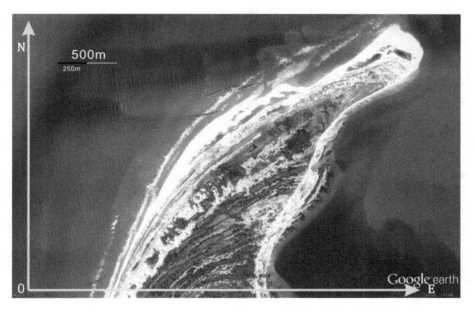

Figure 7-20. *Example trajectories (dark red lines) of GPS drifters deployed on a Florida beach*

Table 7-2. *Example data and results from a student GPS drifter experiment on a Florida beach*

# of deployment	Start point of each deployment		#2 drifter		#3 drifter		#5 drifter	
	Latitude	Longitude	Velocity (m/s)	Angle (degree)	Velocity (m/s)	Angle (degree)	Velocity (m/s)	Angle (degree)
1	29.8753	−85.3989	0.36	250	0.39	253	0.39	250
2	29.8750	−85.4005	0.36	257	0.34	256	0.36	257
3	29.8729	−85.4027	0.32	260	0.31	256	0.36	253
4	29.8569	−85.4128	0.23	244	0.21	245	0.26	243

CHAPTER 8

Working with Pressure, Humidity, and Temperature Sensors

After working with the GPS and SD card to continuously record data over time, we can now start exploring sensors that record weather data. This chapter focuses on using barometric, humidity, and temperature sensors with the Arduino board. Although there are many such sensors on the market, we will use several high-quality yet inexpensive sensors from Adafruit (https://www.adafruit.com/). These sensors are easy to work with, and we will demonstrate how to use them individually before integrating them with the GPS data recorder in the next chapter.

8.1. Tools and Components

The basic tools and components needed for this chapter include those listed in Table 7-1, along with the additional items in Table 8-1. The key components for this chapter are sensors from Adafruit, specifically the

© Chunyan Li 2024
C. LI, *Record Weather Data with Arduino and Solar Power*, Maker Innovations Series, https://doi.org/10.1007/979-8-8688-0814-2_8

BMP280 and BMP390 sensors. The BMP280 is a temperature and pressure sensor that supports both I2C (Inter-Integrated Circuit) and SPI (Serial Peripheral Interface) protocols. The BMP390 is a temperature, humidity, and pressure sensor that also supports I2C and SPI protocols.

I2C and SPI are serial data communication protocols. The I2C protocol requires two nonpower connections: SCL (Serial Clock) and SDA (Serial Data). In contrast, the SPI protocol involves four connections: SCL, SDA, MOSI (Master Out Slave In), and MISO (Master In Slave Out). While I2C allows multiple sensors to connect to the same SCL and SDA lines, it operates at a relatively slower data speed compared to SPI, which can support faster data transfer rates.

Table 8-1. *Additional components and tools used in Chapter 8*

Item	Description
BME280	Adafruit BME280 I2C or SPI temperature and pressure (TP) sensor
BMP280 or BMP390	Adafruit BMP280 or BMP390 I2C or SPI temperature, humidity, and pressure sensor
Four-wire connector	STEMMA QT/Qwiic JST SH 4-pin to Premium Male Headers Cable (for power, ground, SCL, and SDA connections)
Soldering station with some solder	For soldering wires to connect the DC-DC step-down converter to the 2.1 mm DC pigtail male power plug (note: an alternative approach without using the soldering station is to use wire nuts)
Potentiometer (1 kΩ or 5 kΩ)	Need two of them to hook up with the LCD to control the brightness and contrast

(continued)

Table 8-1. (*continued*)

Item	Description
Double pole double throw (DPDT) switch	Optional switch used to disconnect the GPS module, easier for uploading code to Arduino board when GPS module is connected to pins 0 and 1 of the board
Heat-shrink tubes	For insulation after soldering two wires together. Variable diameter heat-shrink tubes should be available for convenience
Heat gun	To heat the heat-shrink tubes for insulation
Standoff (spacer)	Need several, to provide space between Arduino and supporting board, or use as "legs" for the supporting board
Wire stripper	For wire stripping. It can strip wires of different diameters
Micro-bevel wire cutter	For cutting wires – useful for cutting the extra wire soldered on a board
Hook up wire (colored preferred)	22 AWG (roughly 0.65 mm or close in diameter) colored solid wires. These wires are used as jump wires to connect between the LCD through breadboard and the Arduino UNO board
Solder gun	To make connections from the LCD to Arduino, breadboard, and potentiometer
Breadboard	Breadboard for connecting components such as potentiometer, LCD, and Arduino UNO
Electric drill	To make holes to allow wires to go through

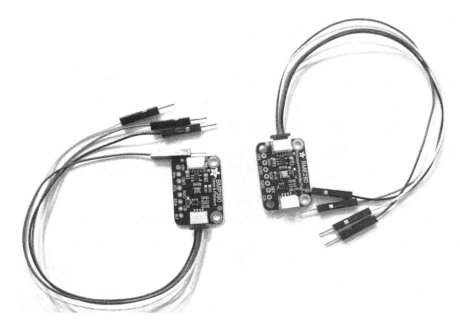

Figure 8-1. *The Adafruit sensor packages BME280 and BMP390. Each of these packages is connected to the STEMMA QT/Qwiic JST SH 4-pin to Premium Male Header cables. The male ends of these cables can be used to connect to an Arduino board or breadboard*

8.2. Working with the BME280, BMP280, or BMP390 Sensor Packages

The Adafruit BME280 temperature and pressure (TP) sensor package and the BMP280 or BMP390 temperature, humidity, and pressure (THP) sensor package (as shown in Figure 8-1), like many similar sensor packages from Adafruit, offer the option to use either a two-wire I2C or a four-wire SPI connection. These sensors also include two additional wires for power: VCC and GND. Since data transmission speed is not an issue in our projects, we will use the simpler two-wire I2C connection for testing. It's important to ensure that the Arduino IDE has the required libraries to work with these sensors.

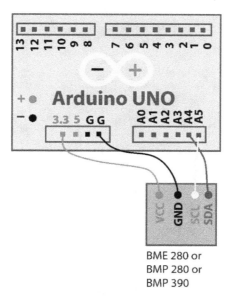

Figure 8-2. *Wiring of a BME 280 temperature and pressure sensor package or the BMP 390 temperature, humidity, and pressure sensor package*

While the wiring instructions and example sketches can be found at `https://learn.adafruit.com/adafruit-bme280-humidity-barometric-pressure-temperature-sensor-breakout`, we will briefly describe how to perform the test here. To get started, we will first use an example from the Arduino IDE.

The I2C connection is simple to implement: the two power wires are connected to the 3.3 V (red) and GND (black) pins, respectively (Figure 8-2). The SCL (yellow) wire should be connected to the analog pin A5, and the SDA (blue) wire should be connected to the analog pin A4 (Figure 8-2), of the Arduino board. In this setup, the VCC can also be connected to 5 V pin.

Figure 8-3. *Choose the example code from the "Adafruit BME280 Library"*

After making the connections as shown in Figure 8-2, start the Arduino IDE and click the "File" menu on the upper left of the IDE, then select "Examples" from the dropdown menu, which will pop up another dropdown menu of libraries. Choose the "Adafruit BME280 Library", and select "bme280test" (Figure 8-3), which will bring up another IDE window with the test program loaded. This assumes that the "Adafruit BME280 Library" has already been installed in the IDE. If not, the user should install the library before proceeding further. Make sure that the board and port are properly selected (you can check them by clicking Tools on the top menu bar of the Arduino IDE). Upload the example code and start the Serial Monitor (from the Tools menu, or press Control+Shift+M); the values of air temperature, air pressure, altitude, and relative humidity will be displayed continuously within the Serial Monitor window (Figure 8-4) if all goes well, e.g., no mistake is made to the wiring. Note again that the baud rate of the Serial Monitor window must match that of the script. In this example, the baud rate was chosen to be 9600. Here are a few lines of the printout in the Serial Monitor window:

```
Temperature = 27.24 °C
Pressure = 1015.93 hPa
Approx. Altitude = -22.28 m
Humidity = 55.51 %

Temperature = 27.24 °C
Pressure = 1015.92 hPa
Approx. Altitude = -22.12 m
Humidity = 55.48 %
```

Figure 8-4. *Showing the measured air pressure, temperature, and humidity in the Serial Monitor window of the Arduino IDE*

The following is the example code:

```
/***********************************************************
  This is a library for the BME280 humidity, temperature &
pressure sensor

  Designed specifically to work with the Adafruit BME280
  Breakout
  ----> http://www.adafruit.com/products/2650

  These sensors use I2C or SPI to communicate, 2 or 4 pins are
  required
  to interface. The device's I2C address is either 0x76
  or 0x77.

  Adafruit invests time and resources providing this open
  source code,
  please support Adafruit andopen-source hardware by purchasing
  products
  from Adafruit!

  Written by Limor Fried & Kevin Townsend for Adafruit
  Industries.
  BSD license, all text above must be included in any
  redistribution
  See the LICENSE file for details.
  ***********************************************************/

#include <Wire.h>
#include <SPI.h>
#include <Adafruit_Sensor.h>
#include <Adafruit_BME280.h>

#define BME_SCK 13
#define BME_MISO 12
```

```
#define BME_MOSI 11
#define BME_CS 10

#define SEALEVELPRESSURE_HPA (1013.25)

Adafruit_BME280 bme; // I2C
//Adafruit_BME280 bme(BME_CS); // hardware SPI
//Adafruit_BME280 bme(BME_CS, BME_MOSI, BME_MISO, BME_SCK);
// software SPI

unsigned long delayTime;

void setup() {
    Serial.begin(9600);
    while(!Serial);    // time to get serial running
    Serial.println(F("BME280 test"));

    unsigned status;

    // default settings
    status = bme.begin();
    // You can also pass in a Wire library object like &Wire2
    // status = bme.begin(0x76, &Wire2)
    if (!status) {
        Serial.println("Could not find a valid BME280 sensor,
        check wiring, address, sensor ID!");
        Serial.print("SensorID was: 0x"); Serial.println(bme.
        sensorID(),16);
        Serial.print("        ID of 0xFF probably means a bad
        address, a BMP 180 or BMP 085\n");
        Serial.print("   ID of 0x56-0x58 represents a BMP 280,\n");
        Serial.print("        ID of 0x60 represents a BME 280.\n");
```

```
        Serial.print("        ID of 0x61 represents a BME 680.\n");
        while (1) delay(10);
    }

    Serial.println("-- Default Test --");
    delayTime = 1000;

    Serial.println();
}

void loop() {
    printValues();
    delay(delayTime);
}

void printValues() {
    Serial.print("Temperature = ");
    Serial.print(bme.readTemperature());
    Serial.println(" °C");

    Serial.print("Pressure = ");

    Serial.print(bme.readPressure() / 100.0F);
    Serial.println(" hPa");

    Serial.print("Approx. Altitude = ");
    Serial.print(bme.readAltitude(SEALEVELPRESSURE_HPA));
    Serial.println(" m");

    Serial.print("Humidity = ");
    Serial.print(bme.readHumidity());
    Serial.println(" %");

    Serial.println();
}
```

In this example, the first four lines

```
#include <Wire.h>
#include <SPI.h>
#include <Adafruit_Sensor.h>
#include <Adafruit_BME280.h>
```

tell the computer to use the four libraries (Wire, SPI, Adafruit_Sensor, and Adafruit_BME280).

The next four lines

```
#define BME_SCK 13
#define BME_MISO 12
#define BME_MOSI 11
#define BME_CS 10
```

define the four digital pins SCK, MISO, MOSI, and CS to be the Arduino pins 13, 12, 11, and 10, respectively. Since we use the I2C connection, these pins are not used (Figure 8-2). The next line

```
#define SEALEVELPRESSURE_HPA (1013.25)
```

defines the average sea-level air pressure which has a worldwide climatological average of 1013.25 hPa (hectopascal, or 100 Pascal, which has the same value as millibar). This value is defined here to compute the altitude of the sensor relative to the sea level, or a reference level. But the reference level does not have to be the sea level, and this reference level pressure can be different from 1013.25 hPa. Particularly, the user can adjust this value if needed to compute the altitude change if the sensor is moving. For example, if a hiker is carrying an Arduino board with a BME280 sensor in operation, the hiker's altitude relative to the elevation at the foot of a mountain (the reference level) can be measured if the above command defines the air pressure at the reference level.

The next few lines define the data communication protocol.

```
Adafruit_BME280 bme; // I2C
//Adafruit_BME280 bme(BME_CS); // hardware SPI
//Adafruit_BME280 bme(BME_CS, BME_MOSI, BME_MISO, BME_SCK);
// software SPI
```

Here, only the first of these lines (Adafruit_BME280 bme; // I2C) is active, i.e., the I2C is used. The other two lines are commented out (not used) but can be turned on if the SPI is used. To do that, the user needs to comment out the first line by adding two forward slash symbols, i.e., //; and uncomment the line needed.

The next line in the script

```
unsigned long delayTime;
```

defines a nonnegative integer for a delay in millisecond between 0 and $2^{32}-1$ or 4294967295. The setup block of the script

```
void setup() {
...
}
```

defines (1) the baud rate (9600 in this case) for the Arduino's serial communication, (2) error message if a working BME280 was not connected or was not connected correctly to the Arduino board, and (3) the delayTime (1 second in this case).

The loop block is very short in this example:

```
void loop() {
    printValues();
    delay(delayTime);
}
```

It implements the operation (measure the temperature, pressure and humidity) continuously and repeatedly prints the measured values using a function printValues() at the intervals defined by delayTime. Since here delayTime is 1 second (1000 miliseconds), the measured values are shown in the Serial Monitor window every second. The function printValues() block is below the loop block.

It has a series of commands printing either strings of text or measured values to the Serial Monitor window. For instance, "Serial. print("Temperature = ");" prints the text "Temperature = " to the window, while "Serial.print(bme.readTemperature());" prints the temperature value after the text, and "Serial.println(" °C");" prints the unit of the temperature (°C, or degree Celsius) and a carriage return with a reset of the cursor to the first character of the next line to prepare another print command after this line of code.

Note that if the test is done using the BMP280, the user should use the example file from the "Adafruit BMP280 Library" (the example file is named "bmp280test"). Likewise, if the test is done using the BMP390, the user should use the example file from the "Adafruit BMP3XX Library" (the example file is named "bmp3xx_simpletest").

If the SPI instead of I2C protocol is used, the wiring needs to be modified and the test script should be adjusted accordingly (comment out the I2C codes and uncomment the SPI codes). For details, the readers should consult the Adafruit web pages (e.g., https://learn.adafruit.com/adafruit-bme280-humidity-barometric-pressure-temperature-sensor-breakout).

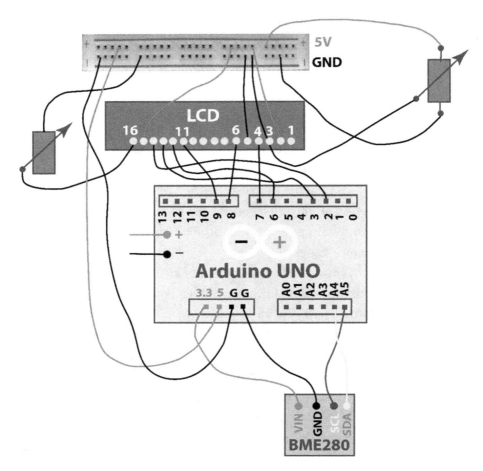

Figure 8-5. *Wiring of a BME280 temperature and pressure sensor package or the BMP390 temperature, humidity, and pressure sensor package on an Arduino UNO with an LCD*

8.3. Display the BME280 Data on LCD

In this section, we will integrate the Arduino UNO, BME280 sensor, and a 20×4 character LCD. We will combine the sketches for LCD from Chapter 5 and the bme280test example from the BME280 library to display

data measured by the BME280 on a 20×4 LCD. The wiring is shown in
Figure 8-5. The wiring for the LCD is the same as described in Chapter 5 so
it will not be repeated here. The wiring of the BME280 follows Figure 8-2.
The integration of the sketches is straightforward, as shown below. In this
integrated sketch, the data is displayed on both the Serial Monitor of the
IDE and the LCD.

```
// Chapter8_test_bme280_lcd2.ino
#include <Wire.h>
#include <SPI.h>
#include <Adafruit_Sensor.h>
#include <Adafruit_BME280.h>

#include <LiquidCrystal.h>
// DEFINE THE CONNECTION OF LCD PINS TO THE ARDUINO PINS
const int RS = 7, E = 8, D4 = 9, D5 = 6, D6 = 3, D7 = 2;
LiquidCrystal lcd(RS, E, D4, D5, D6, D7);  // DEFINE THE
LiquidCrystal AS lcd

                        // ONLY 6 PINS NEED TO BE SPECIFIED
                        // (THE RS, E, D4, D5, D6, D7)

#define SEALEVELPRESSURE_HPA (1013.25)

Adafruit_BME280 bme; // I2C
unsigned long delayTime;

void setup() {
  Serial.begin(9600);
  lcd.begin(20, 4); // DEFINE THE DIMENSION OF LCD
  lcd.setCursor(0,0); // PUT CURSOR AT ORIGIN
  lcd.print("Getting ready..."); // PRINT A MESSAGE
  delay(3000); // delay 3 seconds

    while(!Serial);    // time to get serial running
    Serial.println(F("BME280 test"));
```

```
    unsigned status;

    // default settings
    status = bme.begin();
    // You can also pass in a Wire library object like &Wire2
    // status = bme.begin(0x76, &Wire2)
    if (!status) {
        Serial.println("Could not find a valid BME280 sensor,
        check wiring, address, sensor ID!");
        Serial.print("SensorID was: 0x"); Serial.println(bme.
        sensorID(),16);
        Serial.print("        ID of 0xFF probably means a bad
        address, a BMP 180 or BMP 085\n");
        Serial.print("   ID of 0x56-0x58 represents a BMP 280,\n");
        Serial.print("        ID of 0x60 represents a BME 280.\n");
        Serial.print("        ID of 0x61 represents a BME 680.\n");
        while (1) delay(10);
    }

    Serial.println("-- Default Test --");
    delayTime = 1000;

    Serial.println();
}

void loop() {
    printValues2SMLCD();
    delay(delayTime);
}
```

```
void printValues2SMLCD() {
    Serial.print("Temperature = ");
    Serial.print(bme.readTemperature());
    Serial.println(" °C");

    Serial.print("Pressure = ");

    Serial.print(bme.readPressure() / 100.0F);
    Serial.println(" hPa");

    Serial.print("Approx. Altitude = ");
    Serial.print(bme.readAltitude(SEALEVELPRESSURE_HPA));
    Serial.println(" m");

    Serial.print("Humidity = ");
    Serial.print(bme.readHumidity());
    Serial.println(" %");

    Serial.println();

    lcd.setCursor(0,0); lcd.print("Data Adafruit BME280");
    lcd.setCursor(0,1); lcd.print("Temp. = ");
    lcd.print(bme.readTemperature());
    lcd.print(" C      ");
    lcd.setCursor(0,2); lcd.print("Press = ");
    lcd.print(bme.readPressure() / 100.0F);
    lcd.print(" hPa");
    lcd.setCursor(0,3); lcd.print("Altitude = ");
    lcd.print(bme.readAltitude(SEALEVELPRESSURE_HPA));
    lcd.println(" m");
}
```

Several pictures of the finished product with the Arduino, LCD, and BME280 are shown in Figure 8-6. In this example, I used a real breadboard as a supporting board and cut a rectangular hole to fit the 20×4 character LCD. I also drilled a few holes to mount the Arduino UNO onto the supporting board. A wiring breadboard was used to secure the two 1 kΩ potentiometers. Standoffs (shown in Figure 8-7) were used to create space between the Arduino and the supporting board and to serve as legs. The three-pin potentiometers were plugged into the breadboard (Figures 8-6 and 8-8).

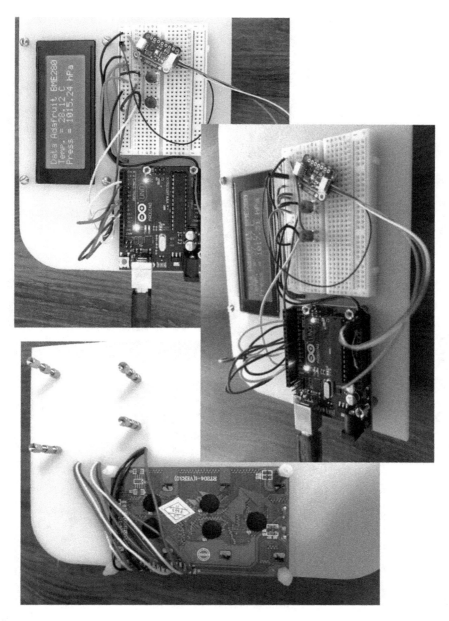

Figure 8-6. *Pictures of front and back of the wired Arduino UNO, LCD, BME280, and a supporting board with standoffs*

Figure 8-7. *Examples of standoffs which can be used as legs for enclosure boxes or used for spacing between the Arduino board or the LCD and a supporting board*

Figure 8-8. *Three-leg 1 kΩ potentiometers*

8.4. Display Both GPS and BME280 Data on LCD

The following sketch for the Arduino IDE displays both BME280 and GPS data on a 20×4 LCD. It combines parts of the GPS sketch from Chapter 7 with the bme280test.ino example from the Adafruit BME280 library. The corresponding wiring is shown in Figure 8-9. When the program starts, the LCD displays

```
Chapter8: GPS+BME280
Read GPS ...
```

with a one-second delay, after which three different screens (Figure 8-10) are shown in sequence with data using a user-defined function getgps(TinyGPS &gps). The first of these three screens show the latitude and longitude from the GPS, the second screen shows the time and dates in UTC, and the last shows the BME280 data (air temperature, barometric pressure, and the approximate altitude in meters above the mean sea level).

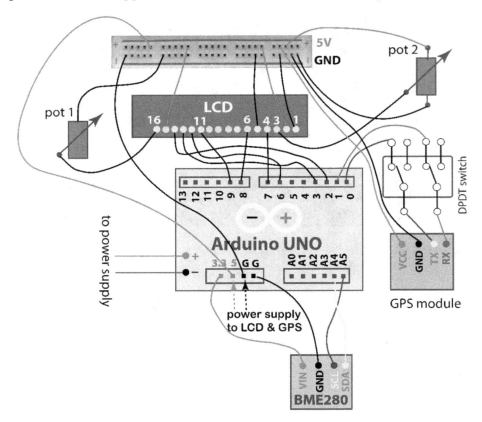

Figure 8-9. *Wiring of a GPS module, a BME280 temperature and pressure sensor package, an LCD, and an Arduino UNO. A DPDT is used*

```
// Chapter8-testUBLOXPGS_TinyGPS_LCD_BME280_1.ino (Figure 8-9)
#include <TinyGPS.h>
#include <LiquidCrystal.h>

#include <Wire.h>
#include <SPI.h>
#include <Adafruit_Sensor.h>
#include <Adafruit_BME280.h>

// DEFINE THE CONNECTION OF LCD PINS TO THE ARDUINO PINS
const int RS = 7, E = 8, D4 = 9, D5 = 6, D6 = 3, D7 = 2;
LiquidCrystal lcd(RS, E, D4, D5, D6, D7);  // DEFINE THE
LiquidCrystal AS lcd

                        // ONLY 6 PINS NEED TO BE SPECIFIED
                        // (THE RS, E, D4, D5, D6, D7)

#define SEALEVELPRESSURE_HPA (1013.25)

TinyGPS gps;

Adafruit_BME280 bme; // I2C
unsigned long delayTime;

void setup() {
Serial.begin(9600); // GPS SERIAL COMMUNICATION THROUGH
                         ARDUINO BOARD'S
                    // DEFAULT SERIAL PINS 0 AND 1
                    // GPS TX --> ARDUINO PIN 0 (RX)
                    // GPS RX --> ARDUINO PIN 1 (TX)
  lcd.begin(20, 4); // USE A 20X4 LCD
  lcd.setCursor(0,0); // CURSOR SET AT (0,0) - 1st column
                        & 1st row
  lcd.print("Chapter8: GPS+BME280");
  lcd.setCursor(0,1); // CURSOR SET AT (0,1) - 1st column
                        & 2nd row
```

```
  lcd.print("Read GPS ...");
  delay(1000); // delay 1 seconds
}

// A function to get GPS data and print to LCD
void getgps(TinyGPS &gps)
{
    unsigned status;

  // default settings
  status = bme.begin();
      if (!status) {
      lcd.setCursor(0,0); // CURSOR SET AT (0,0) - 1st column
                             & 1st row
      lcd.println("BME280 not found");
      lcd.setCursor(0,1); // CURSOR SET AT (0,1) - 1st column
                             & 2nd row
      lcd.print("SensorID: 0x"); lcd.println(bme.
      sensorID(),16);
      lcd.setCursor(0,2); // CURSOR SET AT (0,2) - 1st column
                             & 3rd row
      lcd.print("0xFF: bad address\n");
      lcd.setCursor(0,3); // CURSOR SET AT (0,2) - 1st column
                             & 3rd row
      lcd.print("0x56-0x58: BMP 280\n");
      delay(1000);
      lcd.setCursor(0,0); // CURSOR SET AT (0,0) - 1st column
                             & 1st row
      lcd.print("0x60: BME 280.\n");
      lcd.setCursor(0,1); // CURSOR SET AT (0,1) - 1st column
                             & 2nd row
      lcd.print("0x61: BME 680.\n");
```

```
    while (1) delay(1000);
  }

  delayTime = 1000;

float latitude, longitude; int year; byte
month,day,hour,minute,second,hundredths;
gps.f_get_position(&latitude,&longitude);
gps.crack_datetime(&year,&month,&day,&hour,&minute,&second,
&hundredths);
// print GPS data to the LCD
lcd.clear();
lcd.setCursor(0,0); lcd.print("Lat: "); lcd.
print(latitude,5);
lcd.setCursor(0,1); lcd.print("Lon: "); lcd.
print(longitude,5);
delay(3000); // delay 3 seconds
lcd.clear();

lcd.setCursor(0,0); lcd.print("Time:");
if(hour<10)
{
lcd.print("0");
}
lcd.print(hour,DEC); lcd.print(":");
if(minute<10)
{
lcd.print("0");
}
lcd.print(minute,DEC); lcd.print(":");
if(second<10)
```

```
{
lcd.print("0");
}
lcd.print(second,DEC); lcd.print("UTC");

lcd.setCursor(0,1);
lcd.print("Date:"); lcd.print(year,DEC); lcd.print(".");
lcd.print(month,DEC); lcd.print("."); lcd.print(day,DEC);

delay(3000); // delay 3 seconds
    lcd.setCursor(0,0); lcd.print("Data Adafruit BME280");
    lcd.setCursor(0,1); lcd.print("Temp. = ");
    lcd.print(bme.readTemperature());
    lcd.print(" C       ");
    lcd.setCursor(0,2); lcd.print("Press = ");
    lcd.print(bme.readPressure() / 100.0F);
    lcd.print(" hPa");
    lcd.setCursor(0,3); lcd.print("Altitude = ");
    lcd.print(bme.readAltitude(SEALEVELPRESSURE_HPA));
    lcd.print(" m");
  delay(3000); // delay 3 seconds
  lcd.clear();
}

void loop() {
  // repeating the following actions:
byte GPSdata;
if (Serial.available() > 0)
{
// USE ARDUINO'S SERIAL COMM PINS TO GET GPS DATA
GPSdata = Serial.read();
```

```
if(gps.encode(GPSdata))
{
getgps(gps);
 }
}
}
```

Note that the DPDT switch is an optional item but recommended because it makes uploading codes after revision easier. Without this switch, every time the code is revised, the GPS must be disconnected from the Arduino board. With the switch, we can use it to switch off and on without an error-prone action of disconnecting the GPS the hard way. Of course, we can redefine the serial communication pins and avoid using the DPDT switch (see below).

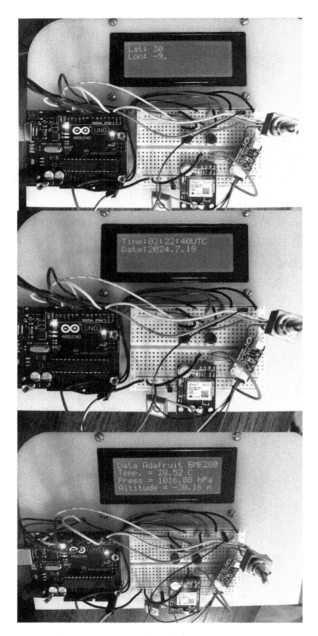

Figure 8-10. *Display on LCD - the three screens shown in sequence each with 1 second delay. Wiring diagram is shown in Figure 8-9*

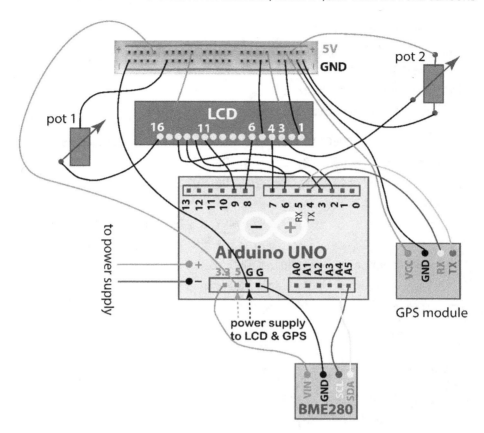

Figure 8-11. *Alternative wiring of a GPS module, a BME280 temperature and pressure sensor package, an LCD, and an Arduino UNO*

An alternative approach is to define different pins for the GPS data in which case the DPDT switch is not needed. The following sketch is modified with a corresponding wiring diagram as shown in Figure 8-11. The sketch is provided below for convenience.

```
// Chapter8-testUBLOXPGS_TinyGPS_LCD_BME280_1_Serial_
pins0&1.ino
#include <TinyGPS.h>
#include <LiquidCrystal.h>
```

```
#include <Wire.h>
#include <SPI.h>
#include <Adafruit_Sensor.h>
#include <Adafruit_BME280.h>
#include <SoftwareSerial.h>

// DEFINE THE CONNECTION OF LCD PINS TO THE ARDUINO PINS
const int RS = 7, E = 8, D4 = 9, D5 = 6, D6 = 3, D7 = 2;
LiquidCrystal lcd(RS, E, D4, D5, D6, D7);  // DEFINE THE
LiquidCrystal AS lcd
                            // ONLY 6 PINS NEED TO BE SPECIFIED
                            // (THE RS, E, D4, D5, D6, D7)
// GPS RX connects to Arduino UNO pin 4
// GPS TX connects to Arduino UNO pin 5
SoftwareSerial mySerial(5, 4);

#define SEALEVELPRESSURE_HPA (1013.25)

TinyGPS gps;

Adafruit_BME280 bme; // I2C
unsigned long delayTime;

void setup() {
mySerial.begin(9600); // GPS SERIAL COMMUNICATION THROUGH
                        DEFINED PINS
                    // GPS TX --> ARDUINO PIN 5 (RX)
                    // GPS RX --> ARDUINO PIN 4 (TX)
  lcd.begin(20, 4); // USE A 20X4 LCD
  lcd.setCursor(0,0); // CURSOR SET AT (0,0) - 1st column
                        & 1st row
  lcd.print("Chapter8: GPS+BME280");
  lcd.setCursor(0,1); // CURSOR SET AT (0,1) - 1st column
                        & 2nd row
```

```
  lcd.print("Read GPS ...");
  delay(1000); // delay 1 seconds
}

// A function to get GPS data and print to LCD
void getgps(TinyGPS &gps)
{
    unsigned status;

  // default settings
  status = bme.begin();
      if (!status) {
      lcd.setCursor(0,0); // CURSOR SET AT (0,0) - 1st column
                          & 1st row
      lcd.println("BME280 not found");
      lcd.setCursor(0,1); // CURSOR SET AT (0,1) - 1st column
                          & 2nd row
      lcd.print("SensorID: 0x"); lcd.println(bme.
      sensorID(),16);
      lcd.setCursor(0,2); // CURSOR SET AT (0,2) - 1st column
                          & 3rd row
      lcd.print("0xFF: bad address\n");
      lcd.setCursor(0,3); // CURSOR SET AT (0,2) - 1st column
                          & 3rd row
      lcd.print("0x56-0x58: BMP 280\n");
      delay(1000);
      lcd.setCursor(0,0); // CURSOR SET AT (0,0) - 1st column
                          & 1st row
      lcd.print("0x60: BME 280.\n");
      lcd.setCursor(0,1); // CURSOR SET AT (0,1) - 1st column
                          & 2nd row
```

```
      lcd.print("0x61: BME 680.\n");
      while (1) delay(1000);
  }

  delayTime = 1000;

float latitude, longitude; int year; byte month,day,hour,minu
te,second,hundredths;
gps.f_get_position(&latitude,&longitude);
gps.crack_datetime(&year,&month,&day,&hour,&minute,&second,&h
undredths);
// print GPS data to the LCD
lcd.clear();
lcd.setCursor(0,0); lcd.print("Lat: "); lcd.print(latitude,5);
lcd.setCursor(0,1); lcd.print("Lon: "); lcd.print(longitude,5);
delay(3000); // delay 3 seconds
lcd.clear();

lcd.setCursor(0,0); lcd.print("Time:");
if(hour<10)
{
lcd.print("0");
}
lcd.print(hour,DEC); lcd.print(":");
if(minute<10)
{
lcd.print("0");
}
lcd.print(minute,DEC); lcd.print(":");
if(second<10)
{
lcd.print("0");
}
```

```
  lcd.print(second,DEC); lcd.print("UTC");

  lcd.setCursor(0,1);
  lcd.print("Date:"); lcd.print(year,DEC); lcd.print(".");
  lcd.print(month,DEC); lcd.print("."); lcd.print(day,DEC);

  delay(3000); // delay 3 seconds
    lcd.setCursor(0,0); lcd.print("Data Adafruit BME280");
    lcd.setCursor(0,1); lcd.print("Temp. = ");
    lcd.print(bme.readTemperature());
    lcd.print(" C     ");
    lcd.setCursor(0,2); lcd.print("Press = ");
    lcd.print(bme.readPressure() / 100.0F);
    lcd.print(" hPa");
    lcd.setCursor(0,3); lcd.print("Altitude = ");
    lcd.print(bme.readAltitude(SEALEVELPRESSURE_HPA));
    lcd.print(" m");
  delay(3000); // delay 3 seconds
  lcd.clear();
}

void loop() {
  // repeating the following actions:
byte GPSdata;
if (mySerial.available() > 0)
{
// USE ARDUINO'S SERIAL COMM PINS TO GET GPS DATA
GPSdata = mySerial.read();
 if(gps.encode(GPSdata))
 {
 getgps(gps);
 }
}
}
```

CHAPTER 9

Integration of Sensors and Solar Power

In the second chapter, we discussed using a solar panel to provide a steady 12 V direct current power supply day and night, along with a rechargeable battery and a solar controller. A step-down voltage converter should be used to reduce the input voltage to the Arduino board, minimizing heat dissipation for long-term deployment. We also worked with the GPS, LCD, SD card, and BME280/BMP390 sensors connected to an Arduino UNO board in the previous chapters. Now, it's time to integrate these components to create a solar-powered device that can continuously record weather data, including air temperature, humidity, barometric pressure, time, latitude, and longitude.

Among the weather data sensors we discuss in this book, we do not include an anemometer, as a digital ultrasonic anemometer can be relatively expensive for most people. However, if cost is not an issue, adding an ultrasonic anemometer should be straightforward for those who have successfully completed the projects in this book. Depending on the model of the digital ultrasonic anemometer, some coding may be required to read the NMEA sentences for wind data through serial communication, which we have discussed in this book.

© Chunyan Li 2024
C. LI, *Record Weather Data with Arduino and Solar Power*, Maker Innovations Series,
https://doi.org/10.1007/979-8-8688-0814-2_9

9.1. Tools and Components

The basic tools, sensors, and components needed for this chapter have been discussed in previous chapters, including those listed in Tables 7-1 and 8-1. To integrate all the components into an enclosure and utilize solar energy, we will need a solar panel, a mounting frame for the panel, a solar controller, a step-down voltage converter, wires, cable glands, and other tools available from stores or online vendors, as mentioned earlier. For outdoor deployment, consider using a plastic or fiberglass enclosure (Figure 2-3) to house all the components, along with tubes for ventilation through the cable glands (Table 9-1). The cable glands should be installed on the enclosure by using a circular saw (hole saw) to create a hole that matches the diameter of the cable gland. The hole(s) should be made on the side of the enclosure, not on the top, to prevent water from getting inside. Readers may need to review these items and ensure they have the appropriate tools for installing the solar panels.

It is also recommended to use a glue gun to secure the electrical connections between the Arduino board and the breakout boards for sensors. The glue can be applied directly, taking care not to damage the connections and not to cover the sensors or your readings may be incorrect. A solar radiation shield can be used to house the weather sensors to avoid direct sunlight exposure. I also suggest using a wooden or plastic board, such as an inexpensive breadboard or a high-quality HDPE (high-density polyethylene) sheet, as a support for mounting the Arduino board and LCD. This makes installation inside the enclosure easier for long-term deployment.

Table 9-1. *Additional materials and tools used in Chapter 9*

Item	Description
An outdoor waterproof enclosure (size ~11×6.5×6)	Housing for the Arduino board, solar controller, battery, GPS module, and sensors
Two cable glands	For protected connections with wire between the inside and outside of the enclosure
A glue gun with glue sticks	For application on the electric contacts between the Arduino board and breakout boards for sensors
Solar radiation shield	To put sensors inside shielded from the sun
Silica gel desiccants	To be used inside the enclosure to absorb moisture
HDPE (high-density polyethylene) sheet or wooden board (~5 mm thick)	Cut to ~10 cm × 15 cm to be used as a support board to mount the Arduino board, breadboard, and components (available on Amazon)
Power drills	Making holes for stand offs or cable ties to fix the Arduino board or the support board inside the enclosure
Cable ties	To secure the support board on which the Arduino board and components can be mounted
Solar panel mounting frame	To securely mount the solar panel to withstand at least normal wind
Clear flexible plastic tube	2-5 mm diameter, 30 cm, used for ventilation to the enclosure for air pressure balance. Installed through a cable gland

9.2. The Wiring, Sketch, and Testing

After completing the projects in the previous chapters, we can now integrate them without much complication in terms of wiring and the associated sketch. The LCD is included in this project for convenience, as it provides feedback or status reports from the Arduino, showing whether valid data is being obtained. However, it is not essential for long-term outdoor deployment. For testing purposes, the LCD is very useful.

If there are no concerns about overheating in the enclosure and sufficient power is available to recharge the battery for nighttime use, the LCD can be retained. Otherwise, it may be removed. If the LCD is removed, the rest of the wiring and sketch do not need to change.

The connection of the LCD to the Arduino should remain the same:

- Pin 1 of the LCD is connected to GND (ground).

- Pin 2 of the LCD is connected to 5 VDC on the power strip breadboard.

- Pin 3 of the LCD is connected to the center line of a potentiometer (POT 2, Figure 9-1).

- Pin 4 of the LCD is connected to pin 7 of the Arduino UNO board.

- Pin 5 of the LCD is connected to GND.

- Pin 6 of the LCD is connected to pin 8 of the Arduino UNO board.

- Pins 7-10 of the LCD are left unconnected.

- Pin 11 of the LCD is connected to pin 9 of the Arduino UNO board.

- Pin 12 of the LCD is connected to pin 6 of the Arduino UNO board.

- Pin 13 of the LCD is connected to pin 3 of the Arduino UNO board.

- Pin 14 of the LCD is connected to pin 2 of the Arduino UNO board.

- Pin 15 of the LCD is connected to 5 VDC on the power strip breadboard.

- Pin 16 of the LCD is connected to the center line of the other potentiometer (POT 1, Figure 9-1).

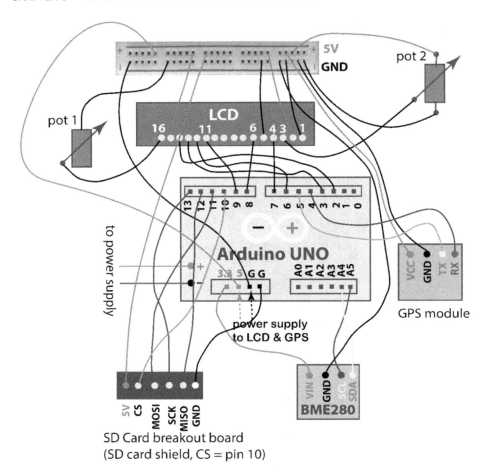

Figure 9-1. *Wiring of a BME280 temperature and pressure sensor package or the BMP390 temperature, humidity, and pressure sensor package on an Arduino UNO with an LCD and an SD card breakout board*

The connection of the GPS module should remain the same:

- The VCC of the GPS module goes to either 5 V or 3.3 V of the Arduino board, depending on whether the GPS module you are using requires 5 V or 3.3 V. Usually, a 3.3 V GPS module can tolerate 5 V.

- The GND of the GPS module goes to the ground of the Arduino board.

- The RX of the GPS module goes to the software-defined TX of the Arduino board – in our case, we use Arduino socket 4.

- The TX of the GPS module goes to the software-defined RX of the Arduino board – in our case, we use Arduino socket 5.

The connection of the SD card breakout board can also keep the same wiring:

- The GND of the breakout board connects to the GND on the Arduino (or the power strip breadboard).

- The CS of the breakout board connects to pin 10 on the Arduino UNO board.

- The MOSI of the breakout board connects to pin 11 of the Arduino UNO board.

- The MISO of the breakout board connects to pin 12 of the Arduino UNO board.

- The SCK (or CLK) of the breakout board connects to pin 13 of the Arduino UNO board.

- The VCC of the breakout board connects to the 5 V of the Arduino.

The connection of the BME280 air pressure, air temperature, and humidity sensor breakout board should be (Figure 9-1) as follows:

- The VCC (red) of the BME280 breakout connects to 5 V or 3.3 V of the Arduino board, depending on the requirement.

- The GND (black) of the BME280 breakout connects to the GND of the Arduino board.

- The SCL connects to the analog pin A5 of the Arduino board.

- The SDA connects to the analog pin A4.

I recommend using a plastic or wooden board as the base for installing the Arduino board, components, and sensors. I have used a plastic breadboard (Figure 9-2), a wooden board, and an HDPE (high-density polyethylene) sheet cut to approximately 15 cm × 10 cm or 20 cm × 15 cm. Drill holes and use standoffs and cable ties as needed (see Figures 9-2 and 9-3) to secure all components inside the enclosure. The reader needs to be creative and base this on the size of the enclosure and the available space for drilling holes, etc.

The Arduino computer code or sketch for the wiring of Figure 9-1 is provided below. Although it is recommended that no changes are made, this design and corresponding sketch have several adjustable items.

First, the Chip Select pin can be modified if needed. Ensure that any wiring changes are consistent with the changes in the sketch and avoid creating any conflicts with other pin assignments. The pin assignments for the LCD can also be changed, but the sketch must be adjusted accordingly. The software definition of the pins for TX and RX can be modified if necessary, but one must ensure no conflicts in pin usage.

The reference ground-level barometric pressure can be adjusted by changing the value (1013.25) in the line #define SEALEVELPRESSURE_HPA (1013.25). Note that we are using a 20×4 LCD. If a 16×2 LCD is used, the sketch needs modification. Use

```
lcd.begin(16, 2); // DEFINE THE DIMENSION OF LCD TO BE 16X2
```

instead of

```
lcd.begin(20, 4); // DEFINE THE DIMENSION OF LCD TO BE 20X4
```

Any command referring to the 3rd and 4th row of the LCD, such as lcd.setCursor(0,2) and lcd.setCursor(0,3), will need to be redirected to row 1 or row 2. Additionally, a delay command can be used to allow each screen to stay visible for a short moment with the defined length, rather than just quickly flashing away. The data file name can also be modified. In this sketch, the data file is named GPSData7.txt.

```
// Chapter9_GPS_LCD20X4_SDCard_BME280_1.ino
#include <TinyGPS.h>
#include <LiquidCrystal.h>
#include <SD.h>
#include <Wire.h>
#include <SPI.h>
#include <Adafruit_Sensor.h>
#include <Adafruit_BME280.h>
#include <SoftwareSerial.h>

const int chipSelect = 10;
// DEFINE THE CONNECTION OF LCD PINS TO THE ARDUINO PINS
const int RS = 7, E = 8, D4 = 9, D5 = 6, D6 = 3, D7 = 2;
LiquidCrystal lcd(RS, E, D4, D5, D6, D7);
// DEFINE THE LiquidCrystal AS lcd
                        // ONLY 6 PINS NEED TO BE SPECIFIED
                        // (THE RS, E, D4, D5, D6, D7)

// GPS RX connects to Arduino UNO pin 4
// GPS TX connects to Arduino UNO pin 5
SoftwareSerial mySerial(5, 4);

#define SEALEVELPRESSURE_HPA (1013.25)

TinyGPS gps; // DEFINE THE NAME OF GPS

Adafruit_BME280 bme; // I2C
unsigned long delayTime;
```

```
void setup() {
  lcd.begin(20, 4); // DEFINE THE DIMENSION OF LCD
  lcd.setCursor(0,0); // PUT CURSOR AT ORIGIN
  lcd.print("Getting ready..."); // PRINT A MESSAGE
  delay(1000); // delay 1 seconds

  bme.begin();

  if (!SD.begin(chipSelect)) {
  lcd.setCursor(0,1);
    lcd.print("Card failed   "); // PRINT A MESSAGE
    return;
  }
  lcd.setCursor(0,1); // PUT CURSOR AT 2ND ROW
  lcd.print("card OK..."); // PRINT A MESSAGE
  delay(1000); // delay 1 seconds
  File dataFile = SD.open("GPSData7.txt", FILE_WRITE);
  // OPEN DATA FILE TO WRITE
                                            // TO SD CARD
    dataFile.println("NaN, NaN, NaN, NaN, NaN, NaN, NaN, NaN,
    NaN, NaN, NaN, NaN"); // PRINT A LINE
      // THE ABOVE LINE IS INSERTED INTO THE DATA FILE EVERY
          TIME THE
      // ARDUINO IS RESTARTED. THIS WILL MAKE IT CONVENIENT
          TO READ IN
      // MATLAB TO AVOID PROBLEM WITH PLOTTING THE DATA WITH
          LARGE GAPS.
    dataFile.close();
}
```

```
// A FUNCTION TO BE USED REPEATEDLY TO GET GPS DATA
void getgps(TinyGPS &gps)
{
  File dataFile = SD.open("GPSData7.txt", FILE_WRITE);
  // OPEN DATA FILE TO WRITE
                                                 // TO SD CARD
  // DEFINE THE DATA TYPES AND NAMES
  float latitude, longitude; int year;
  byte month,day,hour,minute,second,hundredths;
  // GET THE DATA FROM GPS
  gps.f_get_position(&latitude,&longitude);
  gps.crack_datetime(&year,&month,&day,&hour,&minute,&second,
  &hundredths);
  // PRINT THE LAT & LON ON THE LCD
  lcd.clear();
  lcd.setCursor(0,0); lcd.print("Lat: "); lcd.
  print(latitude,5);
  lcd.print("     ");
  lcd.setCursor(0,1); lcd.print("Lon: "); lcd.
  print(longitude,5);
  lcd.print(" "); // delay(1000); lcd.clear();
  // PRINT TIME ON THE LCD
  lcd.setCursor(0,2); lcd.print("Time:");
  if(hour<10)
  {
  lcd.print("0");
  }
  lcd.print(hour,DEC); lcd.print(":");
  if(minute<10)
  {
  lcd.print("0");
  }
```

```
lcd.print(minute,DEC); lcd.print(":");
if(second<10)
{
lcd.print("0");
}
lcd.print(second,DEC); lcd.print("UTC");
// PRINT THE DATE ON THE LCD
lcd.setCursor(0,3); lcd.print("Date:"); lcd.print(year,DEC);
lcd.print("."); lcd.print(month,DEC); lcd.print(".");
lcd.print(day,DEC);
delay(3000);

    lcd.setCursor(0,0); lcd.print("Temp. = ");
    lcd.print(bme.readTemperature());
    lcd.print(" C       ");
    lcd.setCursor(0,1); lcd.print("Press = ");
    lcd.print(bme.readPressure() / 100.0F);
    lcd.print(" hPa");
    lcd.setCursor(0,2); lcd.print("Humidity = ");
    lcd.print(bme.readHumidity());
    lcd.print(" %");
    lcd.setCursor(0,3); lcd.print("Altitude = ");
    lcd.print(bme.readAltitude(SEALEVELPRESSURE_HPA));
    lcd.print(" m");
delay(2000);
// lcd.clear();

  // SAVE THE GPS DATA ON THE SD CARD
    dataFile.print(year,DEC); dataFile.print(", ");
    dataFile.print(month,DEC); dataFile.print(", ");
    dataFile.print(day,DEC); dataFile.print(", ");
    dataFile.print(hour,DEC); dataFile.print(", ");
```

```
    dataFile.print(minute,DEC); dataFile.print(", ");
    dataFile.print(second,DEC); dataFile.print(", ");
    dataFile.print(latitude,5); dataFile.print(", ");
    dataFile.print(longitude,5); dataFile.print(" ");
    dataFile.print(bme.readTemperature()); dataFile.
    print(", ");
    dataFile.print(bme.readPressure() / 100.0F); dataFile.
    print(", ");
    dataFile.print(bme.readHumidity()); dataFile.print(", ");
    dataFile.print(bme.readAltitude(SEALEVELPRESSURE_HPA));
    dataFile.println("");
    dataFile.close();
  }

void loop() {
  // REPEATEDLY DO THE FOLLOWING TO GET THE GPS DATA,
  // DISPLAY ON THE LCD, AND SAVE ON THE SD CARD
byte GPSData;
mySerial.begin(9600);
    if (mySerial.available() > 0)
      {
        GPSData = mySerial.read();
        if(gps.encode(GPSData))
         {
          getgps(gps);
         }
      }
}
```

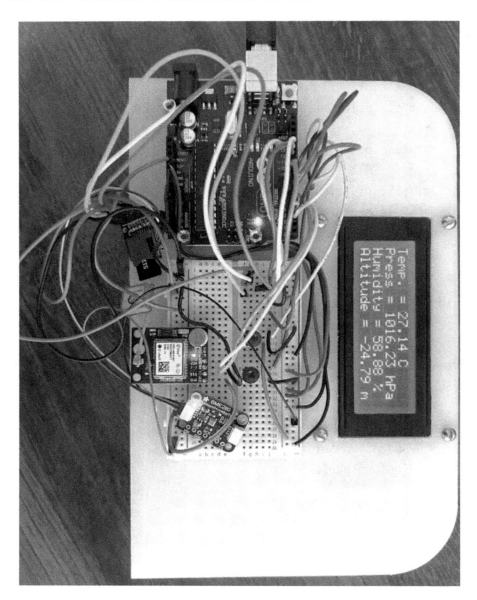

Figure 9-2. *Picture showing the data on LCD using the wiring diagram of Figure 9-1 and the script "Chapter9_GPS_LCD20X4_ SDCard_BME280_1.ino"*

The following is an example data file saved on the SD card using the sketch above for this project. The first column is the year, followed by the month, day, hour, minute, second, latitude, longitude, air temperature (degree C), air pressure (mb or hPa), humidity (percentage), and altimeter (meters).

NaN, NaN, NaN, NaN, NaN, NaN, NaN, NaN, NaN, NaN, NaN, NaN

2024, 7, 19, 16, 6, 39, 30.37169, -91.09028 26.96, 1016.32, 61.58, -25.57

2024, 7, 19, 16, 6, 50, 30.37169, -91.09027 27.00, 1016.30, 60.12, -25.40

2024, 7, 19, 16, 7, 0, 30.37170, -91.09028 27.00, 1016.31, 59.33, -25.45

2024, 7, 19, 16, 7, 6, 30.37172, -91.09029 27.00, 1016.30, 59.22, -25.33

2024, 7, 19, 16, 7, 19, 30.37172, -91.09028 26.99, 1016.27, 59.18, -25.11

2024, 7, 19, 16, 7, 25, 30.37171, -91.09029 26.98, 1016.28, 59.18, -25.19

2024, 7, 19, 16, 7, 56, 30.37171, -91.09029 26.96, 1016.27, 59.23, -25.14

2024, 7, 19, 16, 8, 5, 30.37171, -91.09029 26.95, 1016.25, 59.24, -24.95

2024, 7, 19, 16, 8, 11, 30.37171, -91.09029 26.95, 1016.26, 59.22, -25.04

2024, 7, 19, 16, 8, 19, 30.37170, -91.09029 26.95, 1016.31, 59.24, -25.41

2024, 7, 19, 16, 8, 25, 30.37170, -91.09030 26.95, 1016.28, 59.23, -25.20

2024, 7, 19, 16, 8, 31, 30.37170, -91.09030 26.94, 1016.27, 59.24, -25.08

2024, 7, 19, 16, 8, 39, 30.37170, -91.09030 26.94, 1016.28, 59.23, -25.17

```
2024, 7, 19, 16, 8, 45, 30.37171, -91.09030 26.93, 1016.23,
59.22, -24.81
2024, 7, 19, 16, 8, 59, 30.37172, -91.09030 26.93, 1016.27,
59.27, -25.10
2024, 7, 19, 16, 9, 5, 30.37171, -91.09030 26.93, 1016.29,
59.29, -25.24
2024, 7, 19, 16, 9, 21, 30.37171, -91.09030 26.93, 1016.25,
59.27, -25.19
2024, 7, 19, 16, 9, 28, 30.37170, -91.09030 26.94, 1016.23,
59.25, -24.81
2024, 7, 19, 16, 9, 36, 30.37170, -91.09029 26.97, 1016.26,
59.22, -25.02
2024, 7, 19, 16, 9, 47, 30.37169, -91.09027 26.97, 1016.25,
59.18, -24.96
2024, 7, 19, 16, 9, 55, 30.37169, -91.09027 26.97, 1016.27,
59.19, -25.09
2024, 7, 19, 16, 10, 3, 30.37169, -91.09028 26.97, 1016.26,
59.21, -25.02
2024, 7, 19, 16, 10, 11, 30.37169, -91.09028 26.98, 1016.29,
59.19, -25.29
2024, 7, 19, 16, 10, 17, 30.37170, -91.09029 26.97, 1016.26,
59.18, -25.00
```

9.3. Putting Everything Together and Deployment of Package

After successfully testing the sketch on a laptop, it's time to place the Arduino board and sensors in the enclosure and power them using solar energy through the battery and step-down voltage converter. Before assembling everything into the enclosure, it's recommended to secure the connections between the Arduino board and each of the sensor breakout boards using a glue gun. Apply glue to the pins where there are electrical connections to fix them in place and prevent the contacts from accidentally loosening but try not to cover the pressure sensor, temperature sensor, and humidity sensor by the glue.

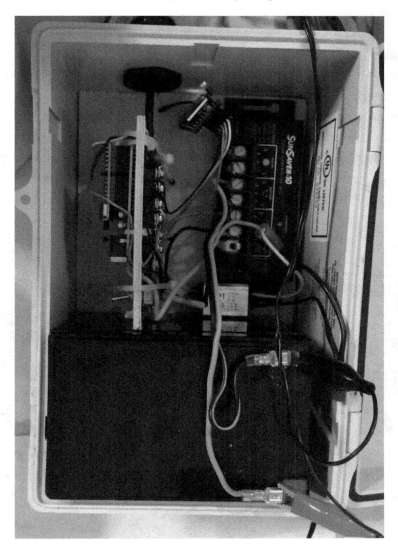

Figure 9-3. *An example of an enclosure housing the Arduino board and electronics*

The enclosure should always remain closed during deployment. It needs to be water-resistant but not fully waterproof, as ventilation is required to allow air pressure to equilibrate with the outside if the air pressure sensor is placed inside. Ventilation can be achieved through a cable gland and a small-diameter tube (a few millimeters in diameter) running through the cable gland. One end of the tube should be inside the enclosure, while the other should extend outside through the cable gland. Leave 15–20 cm of the tube hanging down outside to prevent rainwater from entering the tube.

Place a small bag of silica gel desiccants inside the enclosure for moisture absorption. The ventilation tube should be checked regularly to ensure there is no blockage caused by dust, debris, spider webs, or small insects. The desiccants should also be replaced regularly according to the product specifications.

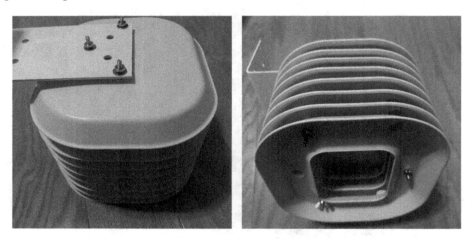

Figure 9-4. *A solar radiation shield. This can be used to shield sensors from direct solar radiation. The sensor package should be put in the central cavity*

Alternatively, the breakout boards for the weather sensors (air temperature, pressure, and humidity) can be placed outside in a separate shielded and ventilated enclosure, such as a solar radiation shield (Figure 9-4). The sensor package should be positioned in the central cavity of this shield. In this setup, an extension cable should connect the sensors to the Arduino board according to the wiring diagram. This extension cable should pass through a cable gland on the side of the enclosure. Ensure that the cable length is not too long to minimize added electrical resistance and avoid using wires that are too thin for the same reason.

A professional solar radiation shield is not required, as a handy person can easily make one. The key principle is to create ventilated housing for the sensors that shields them from direct solar radiation while allowing air to flow through it. This airflow brings in air with the ambient temperature and humidity, which the Arduino records.

Figure 9-5. *Test deployment of a package with enclosure and solar panel*

An example of a simple yet effective solar shield can be made using wood boards. Cut the boards to size, drill holes for ventilation, and shield the box with plastic, wood, or metal sheets. Then, place the sensors inside the shielded box. Alternatively, solid foam with a central cavity (cut out if necessary) can be used and then covered with fiberglass. Covering the foam with fiberglass using epoxy and hardener is relatively straightforward, though it can be messy and requires patience. It's crucial that the fiberglass cover has sufficient ventilation for safety reasons.

Once these preparations are complete, the solar panel and the entire package can be deployed (Figure 9-5), with the solar panel facing the optimal direction (generally south in the northern hemisphere) at an angle that maximizes sunlight exposure. This positioning ensures the battery remains continuously charged and the system runs efficiently for data collection.

Optional: Making fiberglass covers at home requires careful handling and proper safety precautions. Here are some key points to consider:

1. **Materials Needed**

    - Fiberglass cloth or mat

    - Epoxy or polyester resin

    - Hardener

    - Mold release agent or wax

    - Brushes or rollers

    - Protective equipment (gloves, masks, goggles, and long sleeves)

2. **Safety Precautions**

    - **Ventilation:** Work in a well-ventilated area to avoid inhaling fumes from the resin and hardener.

- **Protective Gear:** Wear gloves, goggles, a mask, and long sleeves to protect your skin, eyes, and lungs from fiberglass particles and chemical fumes.

- **Handling Resin:** Follow the manufacturer's instructions for mixing resin and hardener. Avoid skin contact and inhalation of fumes.

3. **Steps to Make Fiberglass Covers**

    - **Prepare the Mold:** Use the object you want to replicate as a mold, and apply a mold release agent to it.

    - **Cut Fiberglass Cloth:** Cut the fiberglass cloth or mat to the desired size and shape.

    - **Mix Resin and Hardener:** Mix the resin and hardener according to the manufacturer's instructions.

    - **Apply Resin to Mold:** Apply a layer of mixed resin to the mold using a brush or roller.

    - **Lay Fiberglass Cloth:** Place the fiberglass cloth or mat onto the resin-coated mold. Use the brush or roller to press it down and remove air bubbles.

    - **Apply More Resin:** Apply another layer of resin over the fiberglass cloth, ensuring it is fully saturated.

    - **Repeat Layers:** Add more layers of fiberglass cloth and resin as needed for the desired thickness and strength.

- **Cure:** Allow the fiberglass to cure according to the resin manufacturer's instructions.

- **Remove from Mold:** Once fully cured, remove the fiberglass part from the mold.

4. **Cleaning and Disposal**

- Clean tools and work area thoroughly.

- Dispose of any waste materials according to local regulations.

Given these steps and precautions, it is possible to make fiberglass covers at home, but it requires attention to detail and adherence to safety guidelines. If you are unfamiliar with the process, it might be helpful to consult additional resources or tutorials specific to fiberglass work. According to my own experience, these homemade shields can last a long time if done properly and deployed securely.

References

Bachmeier, S. (2022). Explosive eruption of the Hunga Tonga volcano. `https://cimss.ssec.wisc.edu/satellite-blog/archives/44252` (accessed 27 May 2022).

Ben-Menahem, A. (1975). Source parameters of the Siberian explosion of June 30, 1908, from analysis and synthesis of seismic signals at four stations. Physics of the Earth and Planetary Interiors 11(1): 1–35.

Blum, J. (2019). Exploring Arduino: Tools and Techniques for Engineering Wizardry, Second Edition, John Wiley & Sons, Indianapolis, pp 512.

Evans, B. (2011). Beginning Arduino Programming (Technology in Action). Apress, New York, pp 252.

Landes, David S. (2000). Revolution in Time: Clocks and the Making of the Modern World. Belknap Press, pp502.

Li, C. (2022). Global shockwaves of the Hunga Tonga-Hunga Ha'apai volcano eruption measured at ground stations. *iScience 25*, 105356, November 18, 2022. `https://doi.org/10.1016/j.isci.2022.105356`.

Li, C., Graziela Miot da Silva, Patrick A Hesp. (2013). Teaching and Learning with New Technology and Excitement: Beach Experiments of Lab-made GPS Drifter with Students, oral presentation at the Association for the Sciences of Limnology and Oceanography 2013 Conference held in New Orleans.

Margolis, M. (2012). Arduino Cookbook: Recipes to Begin, Expand, and Enhance Your Projects, Second Edition, O'Reilly Media, Sebastopol, pp 721.

McRoberts, M. (2010). Beginning Arduino. (Technology in Action). Apress, New York, pp 433.

© Chunyan Li 2024
C. LI, *Record Weather Data with Arduino and Solar Power*, Maker Innovations Series, https://doi.org/10.1007/979-8-8688-0814-2

REFERENCES

Oxer, J. and H. Blemings (2009). Practical Arduino: Cool Projects for Open Source Hardware (Technology in Action), Apress, New York, pp 456.

SiRF Technology. (2005). NMEA Reference Manual, SiRF Technology, Inc.

U.S. Government. (1996). NAVSTAR GPS User Equipment Introduction. Publica release version.

Wheat, D. (2011). Arduino Internals. (Technology in Action). Apress, New York, pp 412.

World Bank, T. (2022). The January 15, 2022 Hunga Tonga-Hunga Ha'apai Eruption and Tsunami, Tonga, Global Rapid Post Disaster Damage Estimation (Grade) Report. The World Bank, pp 41.

Index

© Chunyan Li 2024
C. LI, *Record Weather Data with Arduino and Solar Power*, Maker Innovations Series,
https://doi.org/10.1007/979-8-8688-0814-2

GPSR Compliance

The European Union's (EU) General Product Safety Regulation (GPSR) is a set of rules that requires consumer products to be safe and our obligations to ensure this.

If you have any concerns about our products, you can contact us on

ProductSafety@springernature.com

In case Publisher is established outside the EU, the EU authorized representative is:

Springer Nature Customer Service Center GmbH
Europaplatz 3
69115 Heidelberg, Germany

www.ingramcontent.com/pod-product-compliance
Lightning Source LLC
LaVergne TN
LVHW051638050326
832903LV00022B/802